A VERY SHORT, FAIRLY INTERESTING AND REASONABLY CHEAP BOOK ABOUT STUDYING ORGANIZATIONS

SECOND EDITION

CHRIS GREY

Los Angeles | London | New Delhi
Singapore | Washington DC

First edition published 2005
This edition published 2009
Reprinted 2010

SAGE Publications Ltd
1 Oliver's Yard
55 City Road
London EC1Y 1SP

SAGE Publications Inc.
2455 Teller Road
Thousand Oaks, California 91320

SAGE Publications India Pvt Ltd
B 1/I 1 Mohan Cooperative Industrial Area
Mathura Road
New Delhi 110 044

SAGE Publications Asia-Pacific Pte Ltd
33 Pekin Street #02-01
Far East Square
Singapore 048763

Library of Congress Control Number: 2008924789

British Library Cataloguing in Publication data

A catalogue record for this book is available from
the British Library

ISBN 978-1-84787-342-2
ISBN 978-1-84787-343-9 (pbk)

Typeset by C&M Digitals (P) Ltd, Chennai, India
Printed and bound in Great Britain by
CPI Antony Rowe, Chippenham, Wiltshire
Printed on paper from sustainable resources

FSC
www.fsc.org
MIX
Paper from
responsible sources
FSC® C013604

A VERY SHORT, FAIRLY INTERESTING AND REASONABLY CHEAP BOOK ABOUT STUDYING ORGANIZATIONS

The Author

Chris Grey is Professor of Organizational Behaviour at Warwick Business School, University of Warwick. He was previously Professor of Organizational Behaviour at the Judge Business School, University of Cambridge and Fellow of Wolfson College and continues to hold visiting posts at both of these. Before that he held posts at Leeds University and UMIST and visiting posts at Stockholm University. He is an Associate Fellow of the ESRC Centre for Skills, Knowledge and Organizational Performance at Cardiff/Oxford Universities and is a former member of the Executive Committee of the Management Education and Development Division of the American Academy of Management. For six years he was Editor-in-Chief of *Management Learning* and is currently a European Co-editor of the *Journal of Management Inquiry*. He sits on the editorial boards of *Philosophy of Management, Organization, Critical Perspectives on International Business, Journal of Management Studies* and *Management and Organizational History.* Apart from publishing numerous articles in academic journals, he co-edited *Essential Readings in Management Learning* (Sage, 1994) *Rethinking Management Education* (Sage, 1996), and *Critical Management Studies: A Reader* (Oxford University Press, 2005), and co-authored *Making Up Accountants* (Gower Ashgate, 1998). He currently has an eclectic mix of research interests, including the organization of intelligence and security agencies. He was a member of the DfES's National Educational Research Forum and chaired its task group on research quality, and was Chair of the Management Research Advisory Forum to the National College of School Leadership. He was born in Croydon in 1964 and may well be one of the leading organizational theorists that town has produced.

Dedicated to Alan Grey (1926–2005)

Contents

Acknowledgements to the First Edition

This book has, as an idea, and in the work that has informed it, had a greater history than its length would suggest. In a sense, it represents the culmination of all the years I have been studying, researching, teaching and writing about organizations since 1987 when I began doctoral research at UMIST. Accordingly, I have accumulated a lot of debts, at least some of which I want to acknowledge here.

I have been hugely fortunate over the years to be part of a community of colleagues and friends, many of whom have supported me in personal ways as well as inspiring me intellectually. I can hardly include them all, and those who have been omitted will, I hope, forgive me. They include: Elena Antonacopoulou (Liverpool University), Brian Bloomfield (Lancaster University), Jo Brewis (Leicester University), David Cooper (Alberta University, Canada), Christina Garsten (Stockholm University, Sweden), Glenn Morgan (Warwick University), Martin Parker (Leicester University), Andrew Sturdy (Warwick University) and Valerie Fournier (Leicester University). At Cambridge University, friends and colleagues who have supported me during the time I wrote this book include Sandra Dawson, Peter Fleming, Philip Stiles and Hugh Willmott. I would particularly like to acknowledge David Knights (Exeter University) who taught me more about organizations than I can say. I am also grateful to Kiren Shoman, my editor at Sage, for her willingness to undertake this somewhat unorthodox project, and her unflagging enthusiasm for it.

John Roberts at Cambridge University and Amanda Sinclair at Melbourne University generously gave me comments on parts of the manuscript at various stages, as did Huw Molseed who took on the role of 'general reader' and was particularly encouraging about the project. Anonymous referees read and commented on the proposal for, and first draft of, this book and I also thank them.

At a more personal level, the love and support of my mother, Madeleine Grey, and my wife, Nathalie Mitev Grey have provided a degree of stability in my life without which neither this book nor, more importantly, the work that underlies it could have been completed.

Chris Grey
University of Cambridge, 2005

Acknowledgements to the Second Edition

I am grateful to all those who wrote to me with their comments on the first edition. At least some of you will see that those comments have been taken into account. Madeleine Grey, Nathalie Mitev Grey, Huw Molseed, Amanda Sinclair and Andrew Sturdy have continued to be enormously supportive of what I have tried to achieve in developing this book further. Kiren Shoman at Sage suggested this new edition and has been an endlessly encouraging, skilled and dedicated editor. My new colleagues at Warwick University, and more especially the Industrial Relations and Organizational Behaviour Group, have provided me with a stimulating and supportive environment in which to work. My recent and current doctoral and post-doctoral students have been a constant source of inspiration, challenge and reward – in particular Jana Costas, Juliane Reinecke (both Cambridge University), Sadhvi Dar (Queen Mary University of London) and Todd Bridgman (Victoria University, Wellington).

Chris Grey
University of Warwick, 2008

Should You Buy This Book?

This book is mainly designed for university students who are studying organizations, probably as part of a management course, whether undergraduate or postgraduate. It is not a textbook, and assumes some knowledge of the field. It's also for people who aren't on one of these courses but are interested in organizations and management, perhaps because of their experience of these. And it might also be for academics studying in the field who would like to read an overview of a less conventional approach.

You should buy this book if:

- you're bored by the obese textbook your lecturer has recommended
- you've got the feeling that the textbook stuff is a bit dubious
- you've found that the recommended 'extra reading' is boring
- you'd like to read something stimulating, but not too turgid and worthy
- you'd like to show your lecturer you've done some extra reading
- you want a different take on organizations and management
- you don't want to spend too much money.

You should not buy this book if:

- you want a textbook
- you want bullet points (these are almost the last ones), boxes of text, further reading, further questions and all the usual patronizing stuff
- you're happy to get a minimal pass out of the textbook
- you don't want to have some of your ideas challenged
- you're not too bright at the end of the day
- you want heroic stories about great leaders, fantastic companies and how all is right with the world
- you haven't got even the modest price of the book, or have better things to do with it.

If you do buy this book and want to come back on anything in it, you can e-mail me at: chris.grey@sagepub.co.uk.

Preface to the Second Edition

The first edition of this book was published in 2005, but the bulk of it was written in 2003 and some of the material is even older than that since, as I explain in the Introduction, it had its genesis in a very different book which I abandoned. The idea of a second edition came from Kiren Shoman, my editor at Sage, and was one which I initially resisted. New editions of textbooks are common, as authors seek to keep references up to date. But this isn't a textbook, and in some ways doesn't need updating in that it is a particular *argument* about the study of organizations, and, whatever its failings, this argument isn't really time specific.

Yet the astute reader will perceive that I have, after all, written a second edition, and this for reasons other than having a persuasive editor. On the one hand, I have been both surprised and gratified by how much interest the first edition of the book generated, and I want to reflect upon that, not for reasons of self-aggrandizement but because I think it discloses something of significance about the current state of academic work in the field of organization studies. Most of this preface will be devoted to that. On the other hand, although this is book is primarily an argument about studying organizations, such study can hardly be separated from what is happening in organizations themselves. There is therefore a new chapter on 'Fast Capitalism and the End of Management' which tries to address this. But perhaps that is a disingenuous explanation. What this new chapter probably also reflects is changes in my own position and, in that sense, may in some ways contradict some of the original material. I hope so, anyway, for what could be more depressing than to say, three or more years on, that I have not changed my mind about anything?

One challenge in providing this new material has been that the first edition had a very particular tone and style. Preparing a new edition has made it hard to capture the same tone and style. I haven't tried to do so. But I have taken the opportunity to amend the original text so as to correct some of the grosser infelicities of expression which it contained as well as to make various substantive updates.

So let me now talk about reactions to the first edition, and as a prelude I would like to say something about what I hoped to achieve with it. I felt that there was a space for a book which was neither text-book nor research monograph, and which communicated, to students in particular, something about the gap between what is presented as established knowledge in the former and the way that that knowledge is very often problematized in the latter. I actually had some wider aspirations, too, which the book only partially realized. I hoped that it might be possible to reach an audience beyond students and academics; to appeal to that most elusive of creatures, the 'general reader'.

Perhaps because the book contained an email address and an invitation to make comments, I have had a great deal of feedback from readers – far more than I've received about anything else I've written. Some of this reaction is reproduced on the back cover of this new edition, and it is not just the usual marketing blurb in that probably 90 per cent of the correspondents were positive and a few even said that the book had changed their lives, so the quotes on the book were actually selected from a much larger number of similar comments. A few of those who wrote took me to task for some of the arguments but only one – a student in New Zealand who I will not name, but who may well speak for many who did not choose to write to me – was entirely negative, telling me that the book was irredeemably dull and worthless and inviting me never to write a word again. Charming as her email was, it will be obvious that I have declined her invitation. On the other hand, I may have been lucky not to have had more reactions of this type given that students on many courses are being asked to write essays and take tests on the book, something I never envisaged. I was particularly pleased to receive several complimentary emails from people who were indeed general readers and for whom the main attraction was that the book provided an antidote to the otherwise ubiquitous managerialism to which they were exposed in their working lives. The only consistently negative comment has been about the price of the book. To use the phrase 'reasonably cheap' in the title was always going to be a hostage to fortune, of course, although as I have pointed out to some of those who made the criticism, I don't actually control the price of the book, still less the taxation regimes in force in the various places where it is sold! But this new edition remains the same price as the first, which itself has not changed since 2006, and it has more pages by virtue of new material and a larger font, so I think the reasonably cheap tag is defensible and, if not, then it at least has the merit of demonstrating the contested nature of 'reason'.

Whilst this reaction has been gratifying, it has come largely from an audience I hoped to address. What has been more striking is the way that the book has attracted the attention both of the scholarly community and also of journalists. Amongst the latter, Simon Caulkin of the *Observer* and Stefan Stern of the *Financial Times* both wrote appreciative articles around the book. In the academic literature, there have been reviews in many journals treating the book not simply as a primer for students, but also as containing a serious argument about the nature of the organization theory discipline. Those reviews have been broadly positive – as is inevitable with a book of this sort, some have profoundly disagreed with my fundamental position, a view I can respect whilst of course not sharing. There have also been predictably – and, in fact, predicted in the book – waspish attacks on my attempt at accessibility (for some, perversely one might have thought, the ultimate accolade for a writer is to be unreadable and unread). It is a very considerable temptation to reply to some of these reviews here, at least the negative ones, but perhaps it would be 'unreasonably cheap' to do so.

I would, however, like to pick up on a comment made within the very supportive and generous review from the leading Finnish organizational theorist Janne Tienari (2006). He made the point that many of the examples I use are British, and so parochial. I think that he is right, and I don't think that this new edition is any great improvement on the first in that respect. My only defences are the trivial one that I happen to be British; and the more important point, made again in Chapter 5, that the British case is revealing to the extent that, having been the 'first industrial nation', Britain is also a test-ground for many of the innovations and ideologies of contemporary and 'post-industrial' capitalism. It is still the case, for example, that the politics of former British Prime Minister Margaret Thatcher are invoked in discussions in many countries of how economic 'reform' should (or should not) proceed, a case in point being France at the present time. But I do acknowledge the problem, and apologise for my failure really to address it in this new edition.

The scale of the reactions, and the diversity of audiences from which they have come, and the relatively strong sales it has enjoyed, suggests to me that, despite the flaws and shortcomings the book most certainly has, it has been successful in being seen as 'a different kind of book'. It is difficult to think of many books about organizations which have garnered reaction – still less largely positive reaction – from students, academics, journalists and general readers alike. The reason may be, to coin a phrase, 'fairly interesting' and, so, worth reflecting upon.

The world of organizations, and the way we make sense of them is immensely important because it is central to many, perhaps most, people's lives. But it has been almost entirely evacuated by academics and intellectuals who have any apparent desire to communicate. There are certainly exceptions to this[1] (e.g. Parker, 2002; Sennett, 2006; Ehrenreich, 2006), but from most of us whose job it is to explore organizational life there is little to be heard outside of the stunted and stultifying world of academic journals. One reason for that is the way that, as explained in this book, most organization studies takes place in business schools. This, at least in most 'elite' schools, is a largely sterile atmosphere in which to do work that does not simply reproduce managerial orthodoxy. The general tendency in those institutions is to an ever-more slavish conformity to league tables and rankings (of schools, programmes, journals etc.) which make the possibility of any kind of serious intellectual work, and certainly the expression of heterodox opinion, increasingly rare and difficult. On the other hand, outside of the 'elite' business schools it is certainly possible – indeed relatively easy – to produce work on organizations which is more intellectually engaged and more unorthodox. There are many such schools, especially in the UK, Scandinavia, Australia and New Zealand. And within those schools there are many highly gifted and critically-minded scholars. Yet, despite the existence of this latter group, the business school world is a peculiar one in which the MBA audience, in particular, is by and large exposed to trivialities whilst the academics get on with – well, what? It's a complicated story, in two parts.

The first part is to do with the journals, publication in which is what makes academics' careers. In conventional eyes, these fall roughly into three tiers. The first tier is the North American 'elite'

---

1   It is noteworthy, given what I am about to say about journals, that the examples I have given are all books (and that one of the authors is a journalist). Books do offer a greater possibility for communicative writing but even here the kind of communication I am arguing for is rare, and the textbook and monograph predominate the genre. One reason may be that popular books about management are such a degraded form. But the space surely exists for books – perhaps in the mode of the work of some historians – which are accessible without being unbearably trite?

journals, associated with the 'elite' business schools. These offer little prospect of interesting writing, being largely the preserve of abstract, supposedly scientific, quantitative analysis. Then there is a second tier which is mainly European. In the 1980s and 1990s these journals often carried very interesting work, and some of it is referred to in this book. But in recent years they have to a large extent become obsessed with being recognized by the 'first tier', and as a result most of their articles are dull, formulaic and unchallenging. Then there is the third tier, which is a huge proliferation of specialized journals of very variable quality which allow just about anything to be published: some of it far, far better than anything found in the 'higher tier' journals, by virtue of being freed from their constraints; some of it simply dross, sharing all the defects of the 'better' journals whilst lacking even the patina of professional competence that those journals demand. Readers who are not academics need to understand two things about the world of academic journal publishing. One is that it interests academics far more than anything else because, not necessarily unreasonably, it is what makes or breaks our reputations. The other is that content of these journals, of whatever tier, is neither read by nor, by and large, of interest to anyone outside the academic community, and even then only to segments of it. My criticisms here should not be confused with the relentless call for 'relevance' to which research on organizations and management is constantly, and increasingly, exposed. Those calls inevitably construe 'relevance' as 'relevance to corporate and managerial interests'. My concern is rather with the need to make our work relevant and accessible to a wide range of people with a plurality of interests. And I can say this without, I hope, being accused of ignorance or of sour grapes – although perhaps of hypocrisy – because I have spent much of my working life publishing in them.

Then there is a second part to the reason why organization studies speaks to very few people. It is not just the stultifying impact of business schools or the conservatism of major journals. The intellectually oriented and politically progressive members of the organization studies academic community have increasingly become sunk into obscurantism. Every year a tidal wave of writing is produced about this or that theorist – Lacan, Žižek, Deleuze are current favorites, although the real avant-garde no doubt consider these old hat. The writing style tends to be pretentious and smug; the connection with any concrete experience of work is all but non-existent; the authors rarely offer their own views but simply parade the views of the great theorists before whom they bow down in ritualistic obeisance. This is neither to criticize 'theoretical' writing per se nor to deny the very substantial value of the introduction of a broad swathe of thinkers from other social sciences or philosophy by many pioneers in organization studies, to whom this book is substantially indebted. Rather it is to deplore the recent tendency to do so in ways which obscure rather than illuminate (see Grey and Sinclair, 2006).

So it is within this rather unsatisfactory context that I understand the reactions to the first edition of this book. The establishment is largely moribund (as establishments must necessarily be); what used to be the challengers to the establishment have, not entirely but largely, been incorporated to the extent of being almost equally dull and trivial; the new challengers are too often obscure and pretentious. I said earlier that I didn't want to be self-aggrandizing in speaking of the positive reactions to this book. Having set out the context to these reactions it will be clear that, far from being self-aggrandizing, the main reason why the book was well-received is the parlous state of the field. On the one hand, we have a topic of importance to huge numbers of people, and the subject of study for a considerable section of the student population; on the other hand, we have a group of academics whose job it is to speak about this topic and to these people, but who for these various reasons signally fail to do so.

Let me be clear that it is not my intention to give aid and succour to anti-intellectualism. In the book I make much use of the notion of unintended consequences, and one of the unintended consequences of its reception has been that a few have seen it – usually as misplaced criticism, occasionally as misplaced praise – as giving license to people to avoid difficult or complex ideas (apparently not recognizing that the book itself would have been impossible without the prior existence of a difficult and complex literature; and in a sense the book is an attempt to translate that literature into a more comprehensible form). So to clarify: I certainly don't think that students need do no more than read this little book to have an adequate grasp of the field; I certainly don't think that the way that I have written it is the only worthwhile way to write; and I certainly don't intend my criticism of critical writing in the field to validate bluff, commonsense empiricism or dismissive small-mindedness. On the contrary, I intend the book to contribute to the project of critique, at the heart of which is a politics of transformation and emancipation. To the extent that such a politics ultimately calls for a re-evaluation of dominant ideologies associated with unrestrained capitalism, instrumental rationality and economic growth, the contribution of organization theory is relatively minor, and that of an individual book even less. Nevertheless, if one's aim is to make such a contribution, then writing something that reasonably intelligent people can understand seems to me neither absurdly foolish nor unduly philistine. Indeed, part of a politics of transformation and emancipation must include a serious re-evaluation of the failure of notionally critical academic work (whether or not concerned with organizations) to gain a significant purchase, and to devise new forms for such work.

My original belief that there is an appetite and need for attempts at such forms seems to me to have been vindicated by the reactions, both positive and negative, to the first edition of this book. At any rate, my continuing belief that this is so is what has made me presumptuous enough to inflict this second edition upon the world.

Introduction: Why Studying Organizations Matters to Me

The chief object of education is not to learn things but to unlearn things.
G.K. Chesterton

The purpose of this short book is to say some things about the study of organizations which seem to me to be true. In putting it that way, I am signalling that this is not a textbook, not just because it is far shorter than a textbook but because it has no pretensions to comprehensiveness, and I'm going to assume you've read a textbook or that you have some familiarity with ideas about organizations. Nor is it a specific contribution to scholarship advancing a novel or narrowly defined thesis. Indeed, it is scarcely original at all, except in the sense that the particular things I exclude and the way I put together what I do include are specific to this book. But that kind of originality may be as much a defect as a virtue.

It is, as I say, a short book, and that is for a reason other than laziness or ignorance on my part. The field of management studies, which is where most of the study of organizations occurs, is increasingly characterized by huge, door-stopping, wrist-aching textbooks running sometimes to many hundreds of pages, and also by a proliferation of readers, handbooks and treatises. Whatever merits they may have, they certainly have some serious disadvantages including the physical strain of carrying and reading them. The most obvious is that, in my experience, people don't read them, at least not in their entirety. They are also expensive, sometimes prohibitively so. I wanted to create a book that would fit in the average sized pocket, and not burn a hole in that pocket; a book which could be carried and read on a single longish train journey, say. And I wondered if one way of achieving that was to write in a slightly different way to that which is the norm amongst academics.

Which brings me to my second motivation. Instead of writing a long, comprehensive, scholarly or original book I have tried to write an interesting book about studying organizations – in many ways a more difficult task. Why is it worth undertaking? After all, is there really a need for yet another book on organizations? There are so many already, whether they bear the weighty burden of declaiming the subjects of organizational behaviour, theory and analysis[1]; the advancement of a provocative new angle; or the populist desire to transform the thinking of travelling executives. How many of these are interesting, though, is another question. Many include material which is palpably false. Others announce the blindingly obvious. Still others specialize in the accidentally or wilfully obscure. And all three of these types conspire to be, with a few honourable exceptions, very, very dull.

And yet I passionately believe that organizations are incredibly interesting. In one way, to study them is to study just about every facet of human life. It's true that most of the study of organizations has been concerned with the corporations and institutions where people work, and usually the larger ones at that. But more fundamentally, all forms of collective activity – politics, the family, as well as work – are about organization in some way. Which also means – and it's a major failing of most books to ignore this – that to study organizations involves thinking about philosophy, politics, ethics and much more. And behind or beyond these abstractions are the lived experiences of people not just working together but joking, arguing, criticizing, fighting, deciding, lusting, despairing, creating, resisting, fearing, hoping or, in short, organizing. I don't find it easy to imagine a world without organizations, but I also don't find it easy to recognize that world in the mainstream books about organizations.

If this is so then organization theory – the study of organizations – must also be important. In this book I will talk about both organizations and organization theory because these are so closely related. The way we think about organizations – even to the extent of what we recognize as being an organization – is inseparable from some kind of organization theory. And organization theory has often been used not just to 'think about' but to act within and upon organizations, so that

---

1   I've tried throughout this book to dispense with what the novelist J.D. Salinger called the aesthetic evil of the footnote. But I will just say that all these terms have a currency, contested by scholars. I will use the term 'organization theory' throughout, just to mean the study of organizations. But I don't mean theory rather than practice. Theory/practice is a false distinction. Theory is a practice – doing theory. Practice always involves a theory – some understanding of what is being done and why. But I'll come back to this.

they bear its imprint. So I don't think it is helpful to draw too much of a line between the two and, except where it is important to do otherwise, I won't try to do so.

A more difficult distinction is that between organization theory and organizations, on the one hand, and management on the other. This is partly because management is, in most cases, an interesting and important part of organizational life and therefore of the study of organizational life. It is also partly because, as I have already mentioned, most organization theory is nowadays conducted as part of management studies. Relatedly, it is because much organization theory treats organizations solely or primarily from the point of view of how to manage them (better) – how to get the job done. For that reason, each chapter of this book discusses an aspect of the study of organizations but links this to an aspect of management.

I will say a great deal about this elision between organization theory and management in this book, but for now I will just point out that when organizations are simply thought about in terms of 'getting the job done', it cuts out so much that matters – who says what the job is, who says how it should be done and how are people affected by getting it done this rather than that way? I think that these are really important issues and this book is animated in part by an anger that they are almost entirely ignored by the bulk of organization theory and the huge number of courses in business and management which are offered by universities. But I also think, with less anger but with a degree of sadness, that those people within organization theory who have raised the issues with which this book is concerned have often done so in a way which is inaccessible to all but a tiny fraction of the population. I am not pointing the finger in saying this, because I have done the same thing. But in this book I want to rectify this by communicating something of the more critical[2] orientations of organization theory in a way that those who would not otherwise be aware of them can, without too much difficulty, understand.

It should be easy to write an interesting book about organizations, and difficult to write a boring one. I haven't found it to be so and,

---

2 By critical I mean the growing approach, usually called Critical Management Studies, which explores the kind of alternative understanding of organizations which informs this book, and which should become clearer in the following pages. See Alvesson and Willmott (1992) for an exposition; Fournier and Grey (2000) for a commentary; and Grey and Willmott (2005) for a collection of readings.

most likely, haven't succeeded in doing so. This book has taken a long time to write, even though I've been thinking about it for ages. One reason – maybe an idiosyncratic one – is that every time I tried to write something interesting I felt, as if it were at my shoulder, a hypothetical reviewer criticizing: 'the argument is confused'; 'the author seems unaware of Joe Blogg's groundbreaking paper from last year'; 'the author misunderstands Josephine Blogg's seminal book'; 'theoretically naïve'; 'lacking evidence'; or, worst of all, 'Grey hasn't got a clue – as we have long suspected'.

To placate this imagined reader (who may well have been me), I kept trying, so far as I was able, to refine arguments, close gaps, add references, make qualifications, avoid sweeping assertions. I sought the comments of colleagues, and tried to incorporate them. I worried more about what I didn't know than what I did. In short, I tried to be more comprehensive and more scholarly. So the book got longer and longer, and it was taking longer and longer to write (I'm talking years), which meant that I had to keep reading new material being published. The bibliography took on a nasty, spiteful life of its own. I felt more and more bored by the whole thing. And reasoning that if even I felt bored by it then most readers would surely feel even more so, I threw the manuscript in the bin (today – at the very moment I wrote these words). It's true that it lurks somewhere on my computer – partly as a terrible warning, partly because I might at some point want to write a book that bores me – but I felt the urge to try something different. This is it.

a different kind of book

Imagine a world where the thing which dominated it (God, the Party, Parliament – whatever you want) was written about in one of three ways. One was like a Bible: very heavy and entirely orthodox. The second was amusing and readable but didn't begin to tell you anything you couldn't think for yourself, and never once suggested that the Bible was wrong. The third seemed to say some things you wouldn't think yourself, and suggested flaws in the Bible, but you couldn't understand it because it was so obscurely written.

In that imaginary world you might well feel dissatisfied. In this real world, the thing that permeates just about everything is organizations and their management. You are born in a hospital; you live in a family; you go to school; you go to work. You deal with – what? – supermarkets, banks, mobile phone companies – whatever.

And if you want to understand these things – or, maybe, if you have to because you are doing a management course – then you have pretty much the same three choices as in the imaginary world of the previous paragraph. The textbook that gives you the authorized orthodoxy; the pop management book that you understand but which states the patently obvious and is no more than a better written version of the orthodoxy; or the scholarly book that may challenge the orthodoxy but which is mainly unreadable.

So maybe there is a space for a different kind of book. This is an attempt at it. What I want to capture is something which sometimes comes to me when I am teaching my undergraduate students. They typically know relatively little about the literature on organizations and what they do know they have some scepticism about. But they are intelligent, well-educated and curious. So in class discussions I find myself, on good days, talking with a degree of passion but with relatively little regard for 'the literature', for a 'consistent' theoretical position or for the reviewer on my shoulder. And at least some of my students seem to appreciate that, which makes me wonder if a wider audience, mainly of students but hopefully of others, might also be interested. This book doesn't quite capture those classroom discussions – writing and reading are, after all, different media to talking – but it is written in that spirit. I have given myself the freedom to try to communicate, rather than to obscure. In some respects, the aspiration to write an interesting book raises higher expectations than those incited by a comprehensive or scholarly one. As I have said, I doubt whether I have succeeded, but I have found it more enjoyable than not to have tried. To my scholarly colleagues I offer an apology for the superficiality and violence with which I have treated their ideas, but make a suggestion I will return to: sophistication is sometimes bought at a price which is not worth paying.

people who study organizations

Trying to write an interesting book is one thing, but, going back to the first sentence of this introduction, another set of issues obtrudes. I said that I wanted to write some things about the study of organizations which seem to me to be true. That, I think, will be a perfectly intelligible goal to most readers. It may seem a peculiar or even eccentric goal – why don't I just do some DIY or go the pub like everyone else? – but, given that eccentricity, at least it makes sense.

Yet, curiously and perhaps worryingly, this very first sentence will raise the hackles of just about all of my colleagues whose academic profession is the study of organizations. I think it's worth saying something about this, partly for them but mainly because, for others, it may clarify the purpose, and difficulty, of this book.

Organization theorists – the people who study organizations for a living – come in all kinds of hues. They adhere to a multiplicity of schools of thought which they defend and aggress with remarkable passion. But there are some quite fundamental camps into which many, or most, fall. One distinction is between those who believe that organization theory is, or will become, a science not unlike the natural sciences. It's a loose term, but that view can be described as 'positivism'. Maybe the core of positivism is that there exists an observable, objective organizational reality which exists independent of organization theory. The task of organization theory is to uncover this reality and discover the laws by which it operates, and perhaps then to predict future events. They tend to favour quantitative research. Then there is a second camp, which denies this scientific view. They might be called 'interpretivists' or 'constructivists' or 'relativists', and in their view (or views, for these are not quite identical terms) organizational reality does not have an objective existence but is constructed by people in organizations and by organization theory itself. There are no laws to be discovered and prediction is well-nigh impossible. They tend to favour qualitative work.

One simple way to think of this distinction is to imagine a cricket umpire making an LBW decision or a football referee judging an off-side. The 'positivist' view would be that it either is an LBW or it isn't, and the umpire either gets it right or wrong. The 'constructivist' view would be that if it's called as LBW then it is LBW. One appeals to an objective fact (what the ball did) and the other to a social fact (how it was interpreted by people). Actually, the constructivist might go further, and say that the rules about what counts as LBW are socially made anyway (and so could be, and sometimes are, changed). Note that either of these views can be called 'realistic', the first because it is about what really happened with ball, leg and wicket; the second because it is about what really happened in terms of the batsman being given out and being back in the pavilion. They are just different versions of what might be meant by reality. Perhaps there is also a psychological issue here as well. On the first view the batsman can feel cheated – it wasn't right. On the second view the batsman can feel 'philosophical' – it's just the way it goes.

As this book goes on I will touch again on these debates but for now I want to point out that, from both of these positions, the aspiration to 'say some things about the study of organizations which seem to me to be true' looks distinctly dodgy. For the positivists, the problem is the 'seem to me' part. 'Why should we be interested in Grey's subjective ramblings?', they will complain. 'What we want are the facts of the matter, as established by research.' For the constructivists, it's the 'true' part that is a worry. For them, there is perhaps only interpretation, and to dress this up as truth is an unbearable conceit.

My own sympathies are more with the latter (interpretivist, constructivist) view than with the former, and that is why the truth I am claiming to represent is of the 'seems to me' variety. But I will say to my positivist colleagues and readers who share their concerns that this book is a little bit more than subjective ramblings: it is, or aspires to be, an *argument* made up from fragments of the arguments of others and, if successful, articulated in a way which is plausible to the reader. And maybe that will assuage the constructivists a little, because it means that the truths I am so presumptuously offering are only staking a claim to plausibility, not to objective reality. To the positivists I want to say that the confidence with which they speak their truths is only achieved at the cost of an indefensible philosophical naïvety. But to the constructivists I want to say that the ultimate difficulty with their position is that they can become scared of saying anything at all (not that there is much sign of that) for fear of appearing philosophically naïve. In that case, we might as well all pack up and go home, which might save some paper but would be a shame given the enduring and endemic experience of organization in this and other societies.

There are other kinds of distinctions amongst those who study organizations. I've glossed the positivists as numerically-inclined scientists and the constructivists as description-inclined interpreters (and glossed is the right word). But another distinction which hazily and paradoxically links to this is that between managerialists and critics. The managerialists are interested in organizations from a particular point of view: that of how to manage them more effectively. This also implies that they share the interests, both political (whose side they take) and intellectual (what is analytically important to them), of managers. There is quite a bit of variety here, but these same people are very often the positivists. It isn't hard to see the linkage, for the goal of providing fact-based, reliable organizational predictions would, if realized, be very useful to managers. The paradox, of course, is that the traditional model of science has it as a value-neutral rather than a politically partisan enterprise.

The critics are more concerned with an understanding of the organization as a whole, with some partisan preference for the managed rather than the managers. And these critics are more commonly to be found in the constructivist camp. Because they do not hold out the hope of organizational predictions and control they tend to be seen as less useful to managers. In any case, they are much more likely to question, in all kinds of ways, the organizational status quo. This also means that, because the bulk of organization theory is currently done in management schools, the critics are considerably more marginal than the managerialists. The paradox is also present, in a rather more muted form, for in moving away from the values of management, the critics provide something more like, not a value-free account, but an analytical account of organizations.

Beyond the paradoxes there is an irony. The managerialist-positivist camp, for all their desire to speak effectively to the world of practice, have consistently failed to come up with anything of much use to managers or others, a fact for which they are consistently criticized and over which they themselves persistently agonize. Whereas the constructivist critics at least provide an account which is recognizably about actual people in organizations, rather than the abstract statistical hypothesis testing of their more mainstream colleagues.[3]

Within this axis, I position myself much more as a critic than a managerialist. There are all kinds of reasons for this, which I guess in the end just come down to politics. I don't particularly want to side with the relatively more powerful and I'm sceptical about the benefits of management in the ways that that activity is usually conducted. I think there is much more to organizations than the managerialists typically recognize and, indeed, that the conventional ways of managing organizations represent just one way in which organization could be conducted. In this sense I am, to borrow the words of Martin Parker (2002), 'against management' but 'for organization'.

Throughout this book, I will be conducting a kind of ongoing conversation across managerial and critical approaches. Sometimes

---

3   Compare Vroom's (1964) proposition that motivation M = f(E.V) with the statement 'John would have worked hard for promotion, but as there was no chance of promotion he didn't bother'. Face it, the latter is better.

I will be explaining one or other approach, but more often I will be trying to juxtapose them. Indeed, and this I know introduces some complex problems of exposition, in this conversation I am really using organization theory in two quite different ways. On the one hand, I will be talking about organization theory as a body of thinking espoused in mainstream and textbook accounts, usually of a managerialist kind. On the other hand, I will be using concepts from critically orientated organization theory to illuminate and challenge the conventional wisdom. Hopefully it will be clear at each point what meaning of organization theory I intend, but in any case this problem is an unavoidable result of the fissured character of organization theory. Of course I could just do what most writers do, which is to ignore those fissures and simply write from within one or other camp. But that would defeat my primary purpose, which is to provide for students with a mainly mainstream knowledge of organization theory a mainly critical commentary upon that knowledge. Many others have provided expositions of the mainstream, managerialist approach – almost all textbooks being examples. A few have outlined the critical approach (for example, Casey, 2002). But because they tend to ignore each other, the former do not challenge established wisdom whilst the latter are too far removed from what non-specialist readers already know.

All of this self-positioning is meant to introduce those who are not already aware of it to some of the ways in which organization theory is a schismatic field in which every word used betrays an allegiance to this or that view. Organization theory is itself organized, and it is impossible to write about it without treading on someone's toes. The broad-brush account I have given of its schisms will have done just that for those initiated into these debates. But I would rather make broad, committed (and perhaps occasionally foolish) statements than to become paralysed to unreadability by qualifications and elucidations. I think the *impasse* that organization theory has reached is that those with sophisticated understandings of organizations can only write for each other, whilst those who can write for broader audiences have only the most banal things to say.

To those of my colleagues who may blanch at the liberties I have taken with the ideas that they, and elsewhere I, propound in complex and elaborate terms in – oh, woeful phrase – 'the literature', I say two things. One is that, unfortunately for us, and perhaps for them, almost no one reads the literature. The other, more controversial thing is this: the demand for purity and sophistication is not always a noble defence of rigorous standards, it is sometimes a psychological defence which allows a feeling of superiority over others. It is easy and comforting to see one's own ideas as so sophisticated that any attempt at making them intelligible is to diminish them (and oneself). However, given that organizations are such a pervasive and important feature of life it seems perverse to me that the most important contributions to organization theory can only be understood by a few hundred people in the world – if that many. I sometimes find myself in academic seminars and have the experience of simply not understanding what is being said. If that is true of someone who has spent some twenty years working in the field, who has contributed a fair amount to its literature and, modesty aside, is not a complete idiot, then something is wrong. Wrong with me, perhaps, for not understanding what is said; but as I have got older I have begun to acquire the self-confidence to believe that there may be something wrong with those doing the saying, or at least the way that they say it.

So my intention in this book is to try to say some fairly sophisticated things in a way which is fairly simply expressed. Of course these things are relative: and I am aware that, despite my best efforts, for some this will still seem like a heavy read. There is a certain point beyond which it is impossible to simplify without ceasing to say anything that isn't banal. But I've tried to write in an informal and conversational tone and I have also avoided those textual devices – lists of bullet points, key concepts, text boxes – which, whilst beloved by publishers for their supposed accessibility, I always find patronizing, infantilizing and not even helpful. I've tried to write in a way that demands intelligence, but isn't pompous or patronizing, so those who object on the grounds that it is either too demanding or insufficiently weighty might with great wisdom choose to put it back on the bookshelves right now.

For those who continue with it, I hope this book will leaven the rather stodgy dough of, in particular, the textbooks, and it could be read as an accompaniment to many of these. I have deliberately framed much of the discussion around topics and authors which form the staple of textbooks, rather than introduce some of the more abstruse or obscure theorists (though there's a bit of that) because I want to take some rather tired old material with which students are already to some degree familiar, and comment upon it in ways which hopefully will be a bit fresher. But, to repeat, this is not itself a textbook – if anything, it is an antidote to textbooks – and one difference is that I will not attempt anything like a comprehensive coverage of 'the literature'. Instead, I will mention those sources which I have found particularly inspiring (or, occasionally, particularly loathsome) to say what I want to say.

Another reason for doing some self-positioning in this introduction is to send a certain sort of signal, which the writing style hopefully reinforces. It is commonplace for books, especially but by no means exclusively textbooks, to be written as if their author were absent or, anyway, detached. The first person is avoided or muted, the book is entitled a 'survey', 'overview' or 'introduction'. This betrays a particular way of thinking about knowledge, not unrelated to the issue of positivism. It is as if the author is irrelevant, a reporter on the field of knowledge, not a participant within it. This makes a kind of sense if organization theory is thought of as science, I suppose. But I think of myself not as a reporter or a scientist but as a commentator or conversationalist. So, as I said a moment ago, this book is meant to initiate a conversation, albeit of a peculiarly narcissistic sort in which I am the only one who gets to speak.

where i am coming from

Having so presumptuously put myself at centre stage, I suppose that I should – and anyway that I can – say a little bit more about myself and in particular about some of the things which have informed the thinking expressed in this book. When I first went to university (Manchester, in 1984) it was to study economics. I liked economics because, I suppose, I had been good at it at school and because it seemed to offer a neat and comprehensible explanation of human behaviour. In classes I sometimes asked my lecturers about the way that economic theories always made assumptions, some of which seemed to be dubious, especially those about rationality. Economics seemed to assume that people somehow formed individual preferences (there was no suggestion that these might be learned or that they might reflect the society in which those individuals had grown up) and that they could and did calculate how to maximize the satisfaction of those preferences. I knew from my own experience that people were often not that rational, and I didn't even think that I myself was much like that. I was told that, in due course, these assumptions would be refined. They never were. Instead, economics as I studied it, and I was fortunate to be taught by excellent teachers who represented the best people in the field, developed a more and more sophisticated mathematics to (allegedly) map and predict human behaviour.

Economics is profoundly influential in the study of organizations and management. Many of the core subjects take on board the assumptions of economics – not just, but certainly including, organization theory. Finance, marketing, operations research and economics itself form the bedrock of management degrees. One of the world's most distinguished organizations theorists, Jim March, who over five decades has provided some of the most influential and sophisticated thinking in the subject, wittily remarked that just as economics suffers from 'physics envy' so too does organization and management theory suffer from 'economics envy' (March, 2000).[4] But the consequence of this is that organization theory, like economics, says less and less about the people who I know and who, as a matter of fact, actually inhabit organizations.

Having gone to university to study economics, I was obliged to take some other courses in various social science subjects. Initially, these seemed to me to be a waste of time. Not only did I want to study economics, with a view to being an investment banker (or, rather, merchant banker as it was called in those far-off days), but also I was irritated by the way that so many of these other subjects seems to be concerned with vague airy-fairy debates with no definite answer and, apparently, no real *point*. But I came to change my view quite radically.

At more or less the same time I studied, in economics, Coase's theorem with respect to pollution and, in political theory, ideas about power. I make no pretence to representing either of these sets of ideas accurately, not because I am too lazy to look them up but because I want to capture how they struck me at the time.[5] Coase's theorem, as I understood it, said that if a locality was being polluted then those affected, if they didn't like it, would get together and pay the polluter to stop polluting them. Now in one way this chimed with all that I had learnt about economics; in brief and in general, that the way things were was an outcome of the relative values put upon those

---

4   This tells us something about the field, but also about the people who work in that field. In this book I make it very clear that I am part and parcel of what I have written. In general, though, writers on organizations conceal the way that their own identities contribute to the supposedly objective knowledge they produce.

5   So I apologise if I am doing a disservice either to Ronald Coase or to my lecturers.

things by those involved. But, at the same time, I realized that this account of pollution was, in real terms, nonsense. What if those affected did not communicate with each other? What if, having done so, they could not afford to buy off the polluter?

In political theory I was studying power and, by coincidence (or, who knows, by some clever design of the politics lecturers) there was mention of a study of pollution (Crenson, 1971). This study (discussed in Lukes, 1974, a book I still think of as one of the best things ever written in social science) compared two towns in the US, very similar in all respects except that one had enacted legislation to control a company polluting it whilst the other hadn't. And the explanation of this difference was in terms of the local political set up and power relations between the two towns.

For me, this was something like an epiphany. Economics had offered an explanation that was meant to apply to all people at all times who were faced with pollution. The answer was self-evidently wrong, and in a particular, and very worrying, way. For it implied that if pollution existed then it was because those affected didn't put enough value on the problem to pay to rectify it. This was a fundamentally conservative explanation, of course. Because it said that if there was pollution then it was because no one cared enough to stop it and that if there wasn't it was because enough people were against it to put an end to it. I guess that it was around the same time that I read Voltaire's *Candide* where the character Pangloss enunciated the philosophy (in real life associated with Leibniz) that the way things are is by definition the best possible outcome ('all is for the best in the best of all possible worlds'), a view stingingly satirized by Voltaire. Thus the hapless Candide, subjected to all kinds of sufferings and humiliations, is given 'panglossian' explanations as to why things must be that way, couldn't be otherwise and that, actually, it was a good thing that they were.

By now sceptical of economics, the political explanation made much more sense to me. If similar towns came to dissimilar solutions then I could see that the explanation could not possibly lie in some general calculus of preferences but in how power was mobilized in different contexts with different results. For example, did people see the pollution as a problem and did they think it could be dealt with? More importantly, did the pollution problem ever get on to the agenda of the local authority or not? What influence did the polluting companies have in each case? I could see that these were real issues, whereas the economic explanation seemed to have no reality at all.

I think that at that point I saw things in terms of better or worse explanations of reality, which is not a bad way to look at things. But subsequently I also came to question whether reality was a good enough test. As I have said, I was a student at Manchester in the 1980s and the biggest political issue then was the miners' strike. Ostensibly the rationale for this was a struggle between the economic reality of the unprofitability of pits and the unrealistic demands of the miners for continued employment. I supported the miners on principle and was involved in a very minor way in various activities including the (probably now forgotten) 'Battle of Brittan' when the then Home Secretary Leon Brittan's visit to Manchester was disrupted by student protestors (of whom I was one) and which led to a violent confrontation with the police, which I well remember (somewhat ingloriously, I ran away and hid in a back garden). But at that point I nevertheless believed that it was true that the pits were uneconomic and my objections to their closure didn't include any denial of this, just a concern about its effects and, from what I can recall, a generalized hostility to all things Thatcherite.[6]

But at the same time that I was hiding in gardens, one of my future PhD supervisors, David Cooper was researching in (what was then) the National Coal Board, looking at accounting practices (Berry et al., 1987). He and his co-workers concluded that the claim that certain pits were uneconomic was founded upon particular ways of making the accounting calculation. Make different assumptions and the reality of the economics of the coal industry was different. And the assumptions made were not grounded in 'reality' but in the interests of various different people involved in the industry. Moreover, the release of these research findings was met with a highly political campaign, albeit unsuccessful, to censor and discredit the researchers. I didn't know about any of this until 1987, when I began PhD work, but when I did it made me realize that knowledge itself was political. It wasn't just, as the Crenson study had shown me, that economic calculations ignored political factors, but that economic calculations were *themselves* political in nature.

---

6   Don't ask me to explain how I reconciled this with my desire to be a merchant banker. I don't know whether I knew at the time, and I certainly can't make sense of it now.

I am giving all of this autobiographical detail partly because it helps to explain some of the views expressed in this book. I think that in many ways what I want to urge is a 'political' rather than an 'economic' understanding of organizations. But I have also told this story because I want to explain that the issues I have raised in this book don't come from a kind of 'holier than thou' attitude in which I take some moral high ground. I am – just about – young enough to remember being a student and to remember the worthy, patronizing tedium that I was sometimes subjected to. It's difficult to write a book like this, after years of being an academic, without falling into some of that tone and I know that I have done so. But I do want to try to say that I was once a 19-year-old student, studying economics, not management, but with a pretty similar attitude and set of aspirations to today's average management student. I wanted clear, certain knowledge that I could learn to pass exams and give myself a good career. I didn't give up those aspirations for 'politically correct' reasons, but just because they no longer made sense. I changed my view (and my course).

That was twenty years ago, but I am still preoccupied with how people do things (organizations, politics, whatever) together, and the gap between the realities of this and the way that conventional academic texts describe it. I think that (some) academic ideas help us to understand everyday life and I don't think that there is a world of theory (books, ideas, models) that is dissociated from practice (getting on with things). For – and how boring this will seem – theory is not the realm of abstract theories and practice is not the realm of honest-to-goodness action.

theory and practice

Let me finish these introductory remarks by saying a bit more about that last point. I have come to think that theory is best understood as a way in which people try to pursue particular agendas. Theory is a weapon used to bludgeon others into accepting practice. It almost never reveals that, but still it is true. A good example is the way that Darwinian theory (or, more often, some debased version of Darwinism) is used to justify this or that state of affairs. An example might include the idea that men have evolved to be aggressive and women to be nurturing (I have five sisters, and I can tell you that this is by no means true). Or (closely related) economic theory tells us that the most efficient companies survive because they give better value (never mind that the survival of companies often owes a great deal to their near-monopoly positions – think of Microsoft; or that we often get pretty poor service from companies but the alternatives are much the same – think of banks). So theory in this way isn't separate from practice, it is a way of at best explaining and at worst justifying practice. It is 'panglossian' in that it defends the status quo as being unavoidable or, even, more desirable than anything else.

Now of course theory often advances a different agenda, one for change. But always it is about a change in practice. Fundamentally, theory is about mobilizing ideas, arguments and explanations to try to make sense of practice, but also to influence practice. *See* things differently and you will *do* things differently. No sensible person can say 'well, these are just words'. For we all know that words have the power to influence, to move, to inspire, to hurt and to repel people. Think of how you try to win arguments. Words, as one anonymous saying has it, are loaded pistols: we use them at our peril. Ask any politician and s/he will tell you that the practice of talking is the most important political art. Even – and I'm not much given to seeking biblical authority – the Bible tells us: in the beginning was the word.

And what about practice? Well, this too is invoked rhetorically. The person who says 'well that is all theory but this is practice' is trying to convince you that the practice is better, more worthwhile, more real than theory could ever be (people only say that about theories they don't like, of course). But practice is always based, even if those involved don't know it, on some kind of theory. The husband slamming his fist into his wife's face (the theory, perhaps, women should know their place); the racist beating up an immigrant (the theory, perhaps, whites are superior); or in organizations, the manager making an employee stay until stopping time (the theory, perhaps, people need to know who's boss); or another manager letting a worker go home early (the theory, perhaps, be flexible and people will work harder).

Much organization theory is very closely allied to management practice. It too pursues a particular agenda. It is an agenda which incorporates and validates all kinds of assumptions about organizations, of course, but also about people, politics and ethics about, in short, how the world we live in is organized. I think, and I will explain why in the book, that it does so in a way which is flawed, highly partial, largely indefensible and both morally and practically wrong. I mean, if it did work then it would be wrong, but it doesn't work very well anyway.

what you will find in this book

I'm not going to spend too long on this. After all, the whole point of writing a short book is that people can read it, which is obviously the best way of discovering its contents. But I should maybe give some explanation of what it covers and why.

In the first two chapters of the book I talk about what can be called 'classical' issues in the study of organizations. They are classical partly because they are the earliest contributions to the subject we now call organization theory, but they are also classical because they set out a series of themes, issues and ideas which keep recurring in later work even if in a different language. Sometimes later authors don't realize this, or don't want to (for who wants to hear that their latest thinking just repeats what lies in a dusty corner of the library?). These issues – bureaucratic theory, scientific management and human relations theory – form the bedrock of the knowledge taught on just about every university course on organizations and management. This means that most readers will already have a certain amount of knowledge of them which is helpful to me in my attempt to offer a rather different take on them. And if I can do that successfully then it follows that the same angle can be applied to their recurrence in later work.

In next three chapters of the book I focus on more contemporary issues in studying organizations. As I've already implied, these grow out of, draw upon and sometimes react against the classical work. They also inform much of the experience of work in organizations during the last twenty years or so. For from the 1980s onwards there has been an apparent acceleration of the influence of organization theory in providing at least a vocabulary of, for example, quality, excellence, empowerment, customer service, flexibility and change which impacts very directly upon organizational life. Anyone who has had a job in recent years will recognize that lexicon. Even those students who have never worked will have seen its effects, say in the way that they now complete evaluations of their lecturers at the end of courses. Such a development, whilst minor in itself, arises out of the contemporary issues which I discuss in Chapters 3, 4 and 5. I certainly won't cover all the ins and outs of these issues, but want to deal with their common, central features. Thus I will focus in Chapter 3 on organizational culture, which has not just been a theme of contemporary organizational life in its own right but which is also at the heart of a whole range of other initiatives which position 'values' and their management at the heart of organizations. I will then, in

Chapter 4, talk about post-bureaucracy as a catch-all term for the range of (supposedly) new organizational forms that (apparently) have supplanted the classical ways of organizing by stressing agility, fluidity and change. Again, students will be familiar with these ideas from their courses but, again, I want to offer a somewhat different angle to that normally taught. In the fifth chapter I try to locate recent developments in organizations within a broader context of ideas about 'fast capitalism' in which speed and re-structuring produce a kind of 'rootlessness' with many consequences for individuals and society. Part of what I am suggesting here especially, but throughout the book I hope, is that studying organizations is ultimately inseparable from wider political and social issues.

Since I am making a pitch based on the difference between my approach and that typically found on the courses that most readers of this book take, an obvious question arises. What is going on when what is normally[7] taught differs more or less markedly from what I am saying in this book? One possibility is that I am just wrong, but clearly I think there are better explanations. In Chapter 6 I try to address this by looking at how the study of organizations is itself organized. In this introductory chapter I have talked about this from my perspective, but in Chapter 6 I try to explain what I think is going on in the business schools where, predominantly, the study of organizations occurs. One of the shocking things about these schools is that they rarely have, or impart to their students, any sense of their own nature and purposes other than the claim that they produce better managers – a claim which in my view is untrue. By studying the organizations that study organizations it is possible to understand why the way you study organizations on your course is different to the way I study them in this book. (What was that about readability?) Inevitably this chapter has a slightly different character to the others, because they deal with topics which, one way or another, feature on most courses on organizations. By contrast, Chapter 6 addresses something which is rarely explicitly considered on such courses but which, in my view, should be.

---

7 I should stress, though, that the kind of approach I take in this book is becoming much more common whilst still being in the minority. However, even those who have already been exposed to this type of thinking will hopefully find some points of interest.

Although each chapter is primarily concerned with a set of ideas about organizations, I have also linked these to an idea about management. As I have already indicated, management is not just a part and parcel of organizations but also, in terms of the study of organizations, is often the context and motivation for that study. Organization theory is most often studied inside a management course, and usually by people who are, or who aspire to be, managers. So although there is no necessary conjunction between organizations and management I would be foolish if I failed to talk about the contingent connections between the two. In brief, I associate ideas about bureaucracy with scientific management; human relations with people management; culture with self-management; post-bureaucracy with change management; fast capitalism with the end of management and business schools with the myth of management education. These aren't by any means hermetically sealed notions of management, for there are continuities as well as discontinuities between them. Still, they serve to capture how ways of studying organizations link to ways of conceptualising management.

Finally, conventionally enough, there is a conclusion. But this does more than try to tie things together. Earlier on I mentioned my own passionate conviction about the importance of studying organizations, and I have also tried to show something of the way that that passion was formed. In the Conclusion I want to urge again the idea that all of this stuff *matters*. It is fundamentally about the kind of world we want to live in. We have choices about that, which ultimately means that studying organizations is not just about what I say to you, and that the conversation is not so one-sided after all. All I can do is to bring what I think is true about studying organizations to your attention. In the end, it is your responsibility what you, as students and as citizens, choose to think is true and how you choose to act upon it.

1

Bureaucracy and Scientific Management

*No morality can be founded on authority, even if that
authority were divine.*
A.J. Ayer

The basis of what I will say in this book is the reading, writing,
thinking, talking and listening about organizations that I have done,
originally as an undergraduate student of politics and subsequently
as a PhD student and academic in the area of organization theory. I
keep coming back to the iconic figure in early organization theory,
the German sociologist Max Weber (1864–1920). I mention his
dates because Weber seems to me very much a man of a particular
time. A man of whom it has been said (as it has of others) that he
was the last person to know everything of importance that was to
be known. A nonsensical idea, of course, but one which points to
the extraordinary breadth of his interests in sociology, religion, economics, politics, history, music and much else besides. Nowadays,
in common with other academics, organizational theorists restrict
themselves to a much narrower canvas and this I think gives organization theory a peculiarly detached feeling. For myself, I don't
know where the boundary might be between organization, public
administration and political philosophy; or between organization,
society, family and individual psychology.

And so I like Max Weber for his breadth and also even for his
name, which seems agreeably weighty, Mittel European, *fin de siècle*,
whilst also having the kind of panache that might make it a suitable
name for a twenty-first century architect or fashion designer. I picture
Weber as heavy, bearded, slightly pompous – given to monologues and
pronouncements of the sort that might begin: 'to understand this question we must in fact analyse it under five headings … '. I have no idea
if this is an accurate picture of Weber (although it's true to say that he
did have a beard).

Weber saw that what might hold a society together was some sense of authority – that people somehow submitted to the will of others because they believed those others had the right to give the orders. For sure we could envisage a society just held together by brute force, and maybe much of social organization has this as its origin and, permanently, its background. That brute force – call it coercion, call it power – isn't quite the same as authority, though, which connotes people going along with the will of others through consent given on some basis other than just fear. It's a distinction (probed and criticized by many authors) which runs through thinking about organizations.

Some societies or organizations get held together by the charisma of their leaders: the reason why their will is obeyed is because of their characteristic ability to inspire the devotion and obedience of others. There must be a complex psychology here – bred as much by the followers' desires as the leader's charisma – and most candidates for charismatic authority seem peculiar in both good and bad ways. Jesus of Nazareth and Adolf Hitler might be the two poles. Then again, authority might come from tradition: you obey because that's just the way things are and have always been. The authority of the medieval Church and Royal houses seem like good examples. We can't fully separate out power, charisma and tradition. Inspiring leaders often owe part of their charisma to a propensity to violence; the descendants of such leaders may become imbued with an authority which is purely traditional and, anyway, still backed up with force.

According to Weber, these forms of authority were being increasingly supplanted by something different: rational-legal authority. Here, obedience was secured through a kind of due process: formal, logical, reasoned.[1] Perhaps the key point is that it is not arbitrary – the whims of leaders – but comes from a system. Laws are decided, codified and applied to all citizens. Within organizations, this authority takes the form of rules, procedures and duties. Thus the authority vested in, say, a Chief Executive is of a particular sort. First it comes from the job itself, not the person. We obey (if we do) the Chief Executive because s/he holds that job and not (or not primarily) because of the person's charisma or membership of a particular family. When a new person takes on that role,

---

1   It still had force in the background, of course: disobey the law and coercion follows.

the authority transfers to them. And the role places a limit on what kinds of obedience can be called for. Again, it is not arbitrary. As an academic I can legitimately ask a student to write an essay but not to clean my shoes.

The kind of organization which emerges from the complete application of the rational-legal principle is one which is entirely defined by rules and a series of hierarchical relationships – a bureaucracy. People's jobs were defined: you did the book-keeping but didn't clean the toilets. Then they were refined: you cleaned the toilets on the first floor, someone else did the second floor. And the more the organization grew, the more refined were the jobs. Then again, you didn't do the jobs any old how. What was important was to do them in a way established for you by rules. That way, it was possible to be certain that the job was being done in the most efficient manner. In this sense, rational-legal organization entails the removal of discretion – i.e. judgment or choice – from work. You worked under orders from those above you in the hierarchy and reported to them. The removal of discretion and the fact that authority comes from the role and not the person means that another kind of arbitrariness disappears as well: appointment to a job and promotion were based strictly on experience and qualifications.

Although in many ways not a bureaucracy, something of this process can be seen when, for example, a group of students share a house. Often they will draw up a rota defining who will do chores like cleaning and cooking (all too often a document which experience shows to have been hopelessly optimistic). It defines responsibilities and it is usually animated by some notion of fairness, such that the work is shared equally. It may also be attentive to the particular skills that individuals have (for example, ability to cook). As I say, this isn't a bureaucracy but it shows how even a very simple organization can make use of principles of systemization, division of labour and authority. We would think it odd and, a key point, *illegitimate* if household chores were allocated on the basis of physical coercion by the strongest person.

Weber was by no means a partisan for the emergence of rational-legal or bureaucratic organizations. On the contrary, he seems to have been alarmed by their rapid spread through the state, business and institutions to the point where he feared that the world was becoming enclosed in an 'iron cage' of rationalization. But why were they becoming dominant? Because, says Weber, they represent the most technically efficient and rational form of organization.

what is rationality?

This proposition, its meaning and difficulties seem to me to be defining of a whole set of issues which have resonated through both organization theory and practice ever since. It might almost be said that there is a fault line on organization theory which doesn't just stem from, but runs through, Max Weber. The crucial issue is what it means to be rational. That is a big question and I am not a philosopher (and, in any case, philosophers do not agree on the answer). Roughly speaking, one of the key shifts in human history was that period, around the last half of the eighteenth century, when Enlightenment philosophy emerged, along with empirical science and industrial production. That philosophy was committed to secular rather than religious explanation and the idea that the application of reason rather than tradition or dogma would not only better explain the world but also allow its improvement. In one way, this was extraordinarily emancipating. The philosopher Immanuel Kant, in his 1784 essay 'What is Enlightenment?' (in Reiss, 1991), says that enlightenment lies in daring to know, in having the courage to use one's own reason rather than rely upon the authority of others. This could be said to be *the* foundational text of modern thought.

Yet the rationality envisaged by bureaucracy seems to be the exact opposite of this, for it is precisely the use of one's own reason which is prohibited when the capacity for discretion is removed. Take away arbitrary conduct (which presumably includes both rational and irrational conduct) and you also take away the capacity for the individual use of reason. The rationality of bureaucracy resides in the system of rules, not in the judgment of individuals, except those, usually high up in the organization, who make the rules, and who do retain discretion to some degree. And so from its inception, bureaucracy sets up a dichotomy of systemic and individual rationality.

Max Weber identified another kind of dichotomy. Bureaucracies are rational in one particular sense of the word – formal or instrumental rationality. The idea here is that the means adopted to achieve a particular end are the most efficient for that purpose. This might mean that they minimize wastage and maximize production. And so, although bureaucracy nowadays connotes inefficiency and red tape, its Weberian form suggests otherwise. Yes there are rules, but these are the price to pay for avoiding the calamities that come from not following the rules. Interestingly, current-day attempts to reduce bureaucracy so as to foster innovation frequently run into appalling disasters when, freed from rule-following, organizations take risks which do not come off. Flexibility, too, has its price tag. For Weber, the bureaucracy with its machine-like operation, its complete harmony of individual actions untainted by discretion, could routinely outperform any other kind of organization. Small wonder that it was taking over the world.

Weber's other kind of rationality was substantive or value rationality. Here the question was whether the ends of action were in and of themselves rational. Thus, suppose that I decide to murder someone at random. This is substantively irrational – the end or purpose is irrational, the act of a madman. But if I do so with a swift karate blow to the heart, this is formally rational (it is the most efficient means) despite being substantively irrational. Whereas if I proceed by slapping my victim with a wet fish for several days, then this is neither formally nor substantively rational. Bureaucracies are formally rational but they don't do substantively rational. That does not mean that they are *never* substantively rational, but it does means that they may not be. They simply don't consider that domain of rationality because they are not concerned with ends, only with means.

My murder example sounds like a silly one, but it has a horrifying real-world counterpart in the Nazi Holocaust. According to Zygmunt Bauman's extraordinary book *Modernity and the Holocaust* (1989), the genocide instigated by the Nazis represents the extreme application of a bureaucratic logic. For what makes the Holocaust so peculiarly appalling is the way in which it was conducted industrially – with a system of rules, impersonally applied, which made it as technically efficient as genocide could be. The capacity to register and monitor populations so that Jews, Communists, gypsies, homosexuals and the other categories to which the Nazis were so implacably opposed was itself a considerable administrative achievement. The shipping of these people to the camps was another, and their systematic extermination a third. One of my favourite authors, the novelist C.P. Snow, has one of his characters, a wartime civil servant in London, reflect that, just as he was handling the memoranda relating to the development of atomic weapons, so his counterpart in Berlin would be reviewing figures on the death rate of Jewish people under different dietary regimes (this was written before the extermination programme was known about). Bureaucratic practice, the impersonal, scientific, ethically neutral pursuit of means made the Holocaust formally rational whilst, clearly, not being substantively rational. Bauman says that we should not, therefore, see the Holocaust as an aberration or anomaly when compared with mainstream western culture: rather, it was a manifestation of the habitual ways of organizing within that culture. For sure this is an extreme case, but its logic is very common and is found whenever we detach ends from means – and if it is a case that seems extreme and remote now, remember that it was very real indeed as recently as our parents' and grandparents' generation.

Once we move from the extreme cases, life gets more difficult. For who is to say what is substantively rational? It is a question of values and, whereas there are some values which are so widely shared as to approach universality (so that we can agree about the Holocaust), there are far more cases where there is little or no agreement. This was perhaps not as difficult for Weber as it is for us today. Weber, who had inherited the Enlightenment tradition of Kant, would have hoped that ethics could itself be made the subject of rational judgment. Whereas religions addressed ethics through the authority of tradition, backed up by the not inconsiderable weight of the will of God, post-Enlightenment societies have had to make do with a secularly derived ethics. For Kant, this would be to say that it would be irrational to act in a way which you would not wish to be the way that people generally acted. In other words – do as you would be done by. This still has its appeal, but it (and other attempts at a rational basis for ethics) has real limitations. In particular, people may have quite different views about how they themselves would like to be treated.[2] One of the defining features of contemporary society seems to be a fragmentation of ethics. So substantive rationality turns out to mean a social consensus about values and that consensus does not, to any great extent, exist. We may overwhelmingly agree that that genocide is wrong; we don't agree about abortion or euthanasia.

Anyway, all this aside, the fundamental point is that bureaucracies don't care about substantive rationality, they don't care about ethics, they are just about getting the job done as quickly as possible. That

2   In a high-profile case in Germany a few years ago, a man willingly volunteered to be killed and eaten, and even shared the first course – his severed penis, fried – with the man who went on to kill him. I think we are on safe ground in saying that most people would consider this bizarre, and it does show the limitations of this approach to ethics.

doesn't mean that they couldn't, in fact, be doing an ethically good job (for example, a charity). They could; just as easily as they could be doing an ethically poor one. It's just that this would be irrelevant, either way, to bureaucratic logic. But is this true? One of the most interesting recent books on organizations, Paul du Gay's *In Praise of Bureaucracy* (2000), argues otherwise. Amongst many other points, he says that formally rational bureaucracies do embody a specific and very important ethic. In rejecting patronage and promoting impersonality, bureaucracies are about *fairness*. Being employed or promoted does not depend upon whether you went to the same school as the boss, or the colour of your skin, or whether you agree to sleep with your manager. The service you receive as a client or customer is not conditioned by the mood or prejudice of the person giving the service, or any other value judgments.

This is an extremely important argument. In some ways it is the Inversion of one which has long been made as a critique of science. At least one version of social science (positivism, mentioned in the Introduction to this book) is that it is concerned not with values but with facts. It is neutral. This is another idea going back to the Enlightenment, when the philosopher David Hume proposed that facts and values could be differentiated so that one kind of statement (for example, water freezes at zero centigrade under standard pressure conditions) is a ('positive') fact, whereas another kind of statement (for example, stealing is wrong) is a value judgment (or 'normative' statement). The former are provable, the latter are not. This seems like another version of the formal/substantive rationality split. Science, like formal rationality, is neutral. Substantive rationality is about values. A standard critique of the view that science is value-free is that the idea of value-freedom as desirable is *itself* a value. Yet science has no way of justifying this value. But whereas the *critique* of positivist science is '*so* it does have values', du Gay's *defence* of formal rationality is '*but* it does have values'.

I think du Gay is right in what he says. My only caveat would be that he is only right in relation to what Weber called ideal-type bureaucracies. An ideal-type is the fullest, purest, most complete version of an idea, concept or practice. It doesn't mean that Weber thought that bureaucracies were an ideal to be strived for – as I mentioned earlier he worried about them. But in the pure bureaucracy, there is, as Paul du Gay says, an ethic of fairness. The problem is that actual bureaucracies do not necessarily – and, moreover, often do not – embody this ethic.

▇▇▇▇▇▇ bureaucratic dysfunctionalism

To understand this, I find it helpful to think about a set of classic studies of bureaucracy, sometimes called the 'bureaucratic dysfunctionalist' literature. One of my many objections to organization theory at the present time is its perverse belief that anything published before, say, 1990 – if that – is boring, old hat and that it is somehow shameful to consider it. The fact that many of today's groundbreaking studies do no more than palely repeat earlier work is, of course, no more than a reflection of my old age (I was 39 as I wrote these words). The fact that I have a suspicion that many of the earlier studies were based upon more serious programmes of empirical investigation and thought is similarly antediluvian. But enough of that hobby horse.

The bureaucratic dysfunctionalists suggest that bureaucracies in practice have not just the problem of a deficit of substantive rationality but, even, a deficit of formal rationality. Crozier's (1964) study of French bureaucracy shows how, contrary to du Gay, bureaucrats continue to indulge their own prejudices and preferences in their conduct. They were no more ideal-type that Melville Dalton's *Men who Manage* (1959) who managed to find considerations of gender, race, religion and suburb relevant to their decision-making. Two decades later, Rosabeth Moss Kanter, before she became a management guru, found that managers in a bureaucracy liked to appoint those who shared their own background, gender and education (Kanter, 1977), and this 'homosociality' of recruitment continues to occur in many contemporary organizations despite attempts at equal opportunity and diversity initiatives.

To continue, Gouldner's (1954) investigation of a gypsum mine revealed the presence of 'mock bureaucracy', where an impressive array of rules and regulations, the hallmark of formal rationality, existed. The only problem was that they were ignored. It's common (and this was one of Gouldner's examples) to have safety regulations that staff don't, in fact, respect. A friend and colleague of mine once researched equal opportunities for women in organizations. 'All taken care of', he was told, 'We have a policy' – and a large manual of equal opportunities procedures was proudly displayed. But, my colleague asked, were there equal opportunities for women? Procedures and practices aren't necessarily the same thing.

This idea, that there might be a disjuncture between the formal rules of a bureaucracy and what actually happens, is given an elegant twist in the work of Blau (1955). He noted that one of the most potent weapons in the arsenal of trade unions is the 'work to rule'. Here, workers agree only to follow the letter of what they are obliged to do by contract and job description. Why? To disrupt the organization in pursuit of a union aim, perhaps a pay rise. Yet if *not* following the rules is disruptive, it cannot be the case that following the rules does indeed produce the most efficient of outcomes. There is a gap between the rules and what people actually do that contributes to efficiency and, therefore, formal rules and efficiency are not identical.

Perhaps the 'daddy' of bureaucratic dysfunctionalism is Merton's (1940) argument about 'goal displacement'. Bureaucracies have an inbuilt tendency, because they focus on means and not ends, to degenerate into a situation where the means becomes an end in itself. In other words, following the rule becomes the point, not the point of the rule. Suppose a security guard is taking care of a factory. He (let us assume it is a man) is told to follow a rule, and the rule is that no one is to be admitted without a pass. The purpose or end of the rule is to protect the factory. The means is the security guard checking passes. One fine day the Managing Director arrives early for a meeting. The factory is in trouble and the MD is meeting with creditors. But she (let us assume it is a woman) has not brought her pass. The security guard recognizes the MD, of course, but will not let her enter without a pass. Rules, he says, are rules. So the MD fails to make the meeting and the factory closes down. The security guard's goal or end (protecting the factory) has been displaced, so that the means (checking passes) has become an end in itself. Thus formal rationality swallows up substantive rationality, and systemic rationality overwhelms individual rationality.

formal and informal; intended and unintended

All of these examples and arguments serve to point up two interesting things. Both of them seem to me to be central to understanding anything much about organizations. The first is that there is a disjuncture between the formal and the informal organization. The formal organization of rules, procedures, what is 'meant to' happen, is not the same as the organization itself. The organization itself includes – and in some senses it *is* – what actually happens. This could mean that bureaucracy is less efficient than Weber anticipated and less ethical than du Gay hopes. It means that alongside impersonal rules and procedures we have to consider highly personal prejudices, motivations and actions.

It means something else, too. Bureaucracy has been criticized for dehumanizing people. It is not hard to see why. In the ideal-type, people are no more than parts in a well-oiled machine – devoid of passion, prejudice and personality. Devoid, in a sense, of agency – the capacity to makes choices and act. Yet, for good or ill, this is not so once we recognize the informal aspect of organization. Instead, the recalcitrant or complaining, lazy or hardworking, laughing or frowning, pretty or ugly, trusting or cynical *person* comes back into focus. I will say much more about this later, but for now I will just make one caveat. The formal and informal organization are not unrelated, independent spheres; they are interdependent and mutually constitutive; one could not exist without the other, and the precise nature in any particular case of the one will influence the other.

Then there is a second implication, especially arising from goal displacement. What is done in organizations – for example, establishing rules – will always carry with it the possibility, and, in fact, near certainty, of having both intended and unintended consequences. This idea is a very powerful one. It suggests that whenever people act towards some purpose, the outcomes will be a mixture of what was hoped for by the action and what was unforeseen and possibly undesired. Think of a situation where there are disruptions to petrol supplies. An individual with, perhaps, a half tank of petrol may think it sensible to fill up. But many other individuals make the same (rational) decision. Result? Huge queues at petrol stations, which run out, which causes more disruption to supply and more panic buying and so on. This is an unintended consequence of individual action.

Unintended consequences are perhaps most important when we think about management (and, as I said in the Introduction, that currently is the context in which organizations are most often studied). They mean that the capacity of managers to get things done is often confounded and, moreover, that much of management consists of dealing with the unintended consequences of previous actions. But, since that 'dealing with' will itself give rise to further unintended consequences, this means that management – and organization generally – is perennially failing in the sense that its ends are never finally achieved. Such a prospect means that, other issues aside, the idea of a bureaucratic organization – or any other kind of organization – being simply about the establishment of appropriate means to reach given ends is fundamentally, irredeemably and irrevocably flawed.

These claims run so counter both to the social image of the manager and to what is taught in most management schools (see Chapter 6) that I should elaborate a little more on unintended consequences.

Why do they arise? At least one part of this has already been prefigured. The fact that people have some degree of agency means that it is open to them to ignore, resist, circumvent or just plain misunderstand; all of which will make the best-laid management plans go awry. There has long been a debate in the social sciences about the nature and extent of agency.[3] The so-called structure-agency or structure-action dualism has as its two poles the propositions that social structures effectively determine what happens, and people have little, or no, individual effect or, on the agency side, that all we have is individuals making choices, and social structure is just the aggregate of these. So, for example, debate about crime often polarizes between those who say that crime levels are effectively determined by the extent of poverty, unemployment and social deprivation (structure) and those who see it entirely in terms of individual decisions as to whether or not to commit a crime (agency). Another example would be how we understand the experience of a woman who feels unfulfilled and unvalued because she undertakes childcare rather than paid employment. Is she to be understood as having a personal problem of poor self-image (perhaps addressable through counselling) or a social problem about expectations of women's roles (perhaps addressable through political action)?

Whilst, both in social sciences and everyday life, analysis is polarized between structure and agency, much social theory in the last few decades has, in various different ways, suggested that it is a false dichotomy.

Structure-agency is not an either/or but a both/and. Anthony Giddens (1984), for example, has proposed a duality of structure and action so that action reproduces structure whilst structure conditions and shapes action. The classic example is language. To speak a language in a way that others understand means following the existing rules, or structure, of language that existed before we were born and which we must learn and adhere to. Yet, at the same time, a language only exists because individuals speak it and, as a matter of fact, they constantly adopt new words, slang and ways of speaking, which is why language changes over time. In this sense, language users are agents or actors but they both exist within, and enact, the structures of the language they speak.

---

3   A more challenging issue in relation to agency is the argument that the very idea – usually, of a choosing individual – is itself one specific to modern, especially western cultures. I buy the argument that agency is socially constructed but, given that it is so constructed, its effects are the same as if it were an essential property of human beings.

Thus, in an organization, what people do is certainly conditioned by the rules, procedures and norms prevailing, but these only continue to exist, and develop, because of the actions, choices and behaviours of individuals. Students sit in a lecture hall, following the social rules or structure that determine that they should be there and behave in a certain way and their lecturer similarly follows rules. But in choosing to do this, students and lecturer alike 'reproduce' the social rules or structure through their choice or agency. This seems to me a sensible approach, and it means that agency can never be written out of organizations and so the perfect machine-like organization is a myth. We cannot necessarily predict what people will do.

And there is more to the issue of prediction than simply the question of people's individuality. The added complexity is that people will behave differently precisely because of the predictions which are made about them. This is one of the principle reasons why there is a disjuncture between social and natural sciences (a disjuncture denied by positivists). If I make a prediction about the behaviour of a natural object, it may or may not come true, depending upon how well-founded my scientific theories are: but the outcome will not be affected by the fact of my having made a prediction.[4] But consider something like the housing market. I am thinking of selling my house but want to wait until prices have reached their highest. I read in the paper that prices are set to peak and so put my house on the market. But so do many other people. The result is that there is an increase in supply and prices begin to fall. The prediction has been self-fulfilling. Or suppose I read that prices have peaked and are now falling. I hold off selling my house and so do others. The result is a decrease of supply and prices begin to rise. The prediction has been confounded.[5] There is, in the social world, no way of separating out our theories and predictions about the world from what happens in the world. This is one of the reasons why the predictions of economists, upon which government budgeting is based, so often turn out wrong.

What applies to the social world in general is also true in organizations. Suppose I hear that a new chief executive is being appointed who

---

4   It is worth saying that in the higher reaches of physics there is reason to think that predictions can affect the physical behaviour of objects – but in the everyday range of experience this is not so.

5   This is also another example of unintended consequences, but of a particular sort as it arises from actions in response to predictions.

has a reputation for sacking people. I might decide to look for a new job and leave before I am fired. I might decide to work very hard in the hope that the axe will fall elsewhere. I might decide to work less hard as I think I am likely to lose my job anyway. Predictions about the future change conduct and therefore affect just what happens in the future. In a similar way, assumptions about people can have strange effects. I will talk more about this later, but, for now, consider the case of a manager who assumes that the workforce is motivated by money. Accordingly, a pay system is devised with, for example, bonuses for good performance. In these circumstances the assumption is likely to be self-fulfilling in that the workforce, offered only the motivation of money, will be motivated only by money. Their commitment to the quality of work or the company itself will be limited or non-existent.

An important factor implicit in all this is that organizations, like life in general, take place in time. We cannot imagine an equilibrium point. Continuing my previous example, suppose in response to a materialistic workforce a new human resource manager is appointed. She thinks the answer is to give the workforce more freedom and responsibility. Some of them, used to the previous style, respond by taking advantage of this to slack off. In the meantime, others leave and are replaced by people who have only known the new system. But by now the slackers are a problem and the manager tightens up. The new workers are now resentful. But anyhow, by now the company has been taken over and a new management system is being introduced – and so it continues. There is no one point at which a supposedly optimum system of organization can be reached and, again, this means that the solutions to problems at any one time form the basis of new problems in the future. This dynamic, temporal character of organizations is again a reason for plans being confounded and unintended consequences arising. In this sense, rather than thinking about organizations as fixed entities, it might be better to think of them as current manifestations of an ongoing process of *organizing*.

These kinds of issues – agency, unpredictability, goal displacement and, overall, unintended consequences – are the irreducible core of organization. They are not anomalies. For example, in the British education system, attempts are made to set targets for attainment. It might be that schools should achieve a 25 per cent target for A–C grades in GCSE. The purpose is to ensure that all pupils, not just the highest achievers, are catered for. But consider the school at 23 per cent. There the teacher's best hope of reaching the target is to concentrate effort on the 2 per cent of the class falling just outside the target and to neglect everyone else (see Gewirtz, 2002, for detail). So wider educational attainment has been lost in pursuit of a specific target. Or, in the NHS, attempts to shorten waiting lists by introducing target times have been confounded by hospitals creating waiting lists for waiting lists and thereby meeting the target. These are all recognizable cases of unintended consequences, goal displacement and the over-run of substantive rationality by formal rationality. Yet the irony is that these effects are then treated as a new problem, demanding new targets, new measures, new ways of organizing, which then go on to create their own unintended consequences. It is in this sense that organizations and management are perennially failing.

so what?

I suppose that there is a big 'so what?' to all of this. After all, if this is true, what are we to do? Just give up trying to organize? That seems tricky if organization is in some way endemic to human culture. Perhaps we just have to accept unintended consequences and get on with it if there is no alternative. I don't have any straightforward answers to this but, at the very least, I think that simply to recognize the issues takes us a long way forward. First off, it might call forth a degree of humility from, in particular, managers and politicians. Too often they act as if they can deliver perfect solutions. Relatedly, it suggests the need for a degree of care. Unintended consequences may always be with us, but some are more foreseeable than others. Confronted with a problem, managers often too quickly and too confidently announce that the answer is simple: a reorganization; a new inventory system; a new accounting system; a new reward system. This is a conceit often fed by management consultants, gurus and business schools. Encountering a call for more deliberation, the response will typically be that there is no time to do so – but this is surely irresponsible, and to some large extent the busy-ness of managers is simply self-perpetuating, for in a sense it accelerates time. Additionally, and related to time, one feature of managerial careers is that people have often moved jobs before the unintended consequences they have created become manifest. This in itself is a recipe for irresponsibility (one might say it is an unintended consequence of the design of managerial careers).

However, there are much wider implications for what I have tried to say so far in this chapter. Ultimately, we cannot conceive of a form of organization and management in which means are detached from ends (and I mean here both goals and effects, both intended and unintended). For this is to detach organization from ethics and values. In the Introduction to this book I said that my approach to organization theory is in some ways 'anti-management', and the ultimate reason for this is that it seems to me that much or most writing on organizations and management does purport to detach means from ends and does ignore, or significantly truncate, attention to ethics and values. I want now to elaborate that thought a bit more, this time by talking about some of the origins of management thought and practice, origins which have left an enduring legacy to the present day.

taylorism and scientific management

To do this, I will introduce another of the iconic figures from organization theory, from a similar time to Max Weber, but a man of a very different stamp: Frederick Winslow Taylor. Taylor (1856–1917) was no theorist, he was an engineer working in one of the toughest of industries (iron and steelmaking) during one of the most remarkable periods of technical and managerial innovation the world has seen: the industrialization of the United States following the American Civil War. In one way, it was remarkable that Taylor was doing this job at all. Born into a wealthy Philadelphia family, he seemed destined for a career in the law when he took the unusual decision to go into the steel business, initially as an apprentice. His childhood had been rigidly controlled, with all his activities – sport, walking, sleeping position and country dancing – minutely analysed and prescribed (Fineman, 1996: 545).

This might lead us to understand his life's work in primarily psychological terms, but this would be mistaken to the extent that it was also historically rooted (structure and agency again). For one thing that is worth saying at the outset is that a great many other people, many of them engineers, were developing similar ideas to Taylor at a similar time in a similar place. But it is Taylor's name that has become inseparable from this general movement, usually known as 'scientific management'. By recognizing that this *was* a general movement, it is possible to see that it reflected a particular set of problems, assumptions and attitudes; it did not emerge by chance, and its context is really quite important.

Pennsylvania in and around the 1870s was a revolutionary place.[6] Its smokestacks bore testament to industry on a scale and pace that had never been seen before, even in the English Industrial Revolution. It is almost no exaggeration to say that it was out of this cockpit that management, and a good part of what has defined human society since, at least in the West, emerged. It did so in a form which gave management what Yehouda Shenhav (1999), in one of the finest historical studies of the subject, has called its engineering legacy. It is no coincidence (as I will discuss in Chapter 6) that it was also in Pennsylvania that the world's first business school, Wharton, was founded in 1881, nor that Joseph Wharton was both the founder of that school and the owner of one of Taylor's workplaces.

The steel industry (and others) was in large part the creation of immigrants and in ways which had an interesting pattern, right from the beginning. The mill owners and many of the engineers were often from Scottish families and were often (like Taylor) Protestant or Nonconformist in religion. Weber knew all about Taylor, and regarded his work as emblematic of the advance of rationalized organization. And Weber had also advanced the thesis that Protestantism, with its values of thrift, hard work and individualism, had a peculiar affinity with the development of capitalism. The US steel industry bore this out. The workers in the mills, however, typically had a different background. In the early years, they were more likely to be Irish emigrants and to be Catholics. Later, they came from all parts of Europe and spoke a Babel of languages. It is no small part of the context of scientific management that it emerged as an artefact to the relationship between Protestants and Catholics and English and non-English speakers: it is overlaid by cultural and racial assumptions. It's also worth saying that steel was an overwhelmingly male, and even macho, industry, and this too left its mark on management.

Taylor (I'll cease from now on to remember others doing the same thing) identified a problem based on his early experience as a machine operator. He was working in some of the biggest of the iron and steel plants, at Midvale and Bethlehem (this was the one owned by Joseph Wharton) in Pennsylvania, and his problem was one which is familiar to anyone who, like me, knows nothing about cars. When I go to the garage to have my car fixed, the mechanic may say to me – sucking in

---

6   Its modern-day equivalents might be the massively growing heavy industry of China or the call centres of India. Such locations exhibit many of the techniques developed by Taylor but they also share the sense of being places where the world is being re-made.

air through his[7] teeth – that I have a serious problem, that it will take several days to fix, and that it will cost me a large amount of money. I have no way of knowing if this is true. I don't know what the fault is, I don't know if it could be fixed more quickly, I don't know what parts will be needed. What I do about all this will in large part depend upon the extent to which I trust the mechanic.

Taylor's problem was similar. He was working in an industry where it was normal for workers to organize their own work. Work gangs hired their own crew, worked at their own pace, used their own tools and, crucially, knew far more about the work than did their supervisors. Work was assigned and done on a rule of thumb or 'guesstimate' basis. Taylor reckoned that workers tended to, as he called it, 'soldier'; he meant that they slacked off, either because of 'natural soldiering' – they were naturally lazy and would work as little as they could – or 'systematic soldiering' – they would deliberately restrict output so as to keep their jobs and maximize staff levels for themselves and their friends. It's noticeable that this implies that Taylor didn't trust the workers much, and here the cultural context is important: it reflects in part the stereotypical attitude of work ethic Puritans towards the supposedly feckless and dishonest Catholics.

The solution lay in scientific management, which Taylor articulated in many different ways but most famously in his four principles, familiar no doubt to every student of management and organizations:

- A science of each element of work.
- Scientific selection and training of workers.
- Division of labour between workers and managers.
- Co-operation between managers and workers.

In practice what the first of these meant was time and motion (T&M) studies. T&M meant managers using a stopwatch and standing over a worker to measure what the time taken for each tiny component of the job being done. Imagine the act of drinking a glass of beer:

Start position: Standing at bar
Movement 1: Hand to glass (2 seconds)
Movement 2: Grip glass (0.5 seconds)
Movement 3: Lift to horizontal (1 second)

---

7   Yes, I know. But most mechanics are male, aren't they?

Movement 4: Lift to lips (1 second)
Movement 5: Swallow 0.05 litres beer (2 seconds)
Movement 6: Move arm to horizontal (1 second)
Movement 7: Move glass to bar (1 second)
Movement 8: Release grip on glass (0.5 seconds)
Movement 9: Belch (1 second)
End position: Standing at bar
Total time for operation: 10 seconds

In practice, of course, it would be an industrial process operation but the principle is the same. It establishes the optimum time for the operation with no wastage (from the point of view of the operation itself) with other activities: no pausing to smile, or pick up a cigarette, or pop to the loo or eye-up the person next to you at the bar. It is easy to see why this technique attracted Weber's attention, for it is an exemplar of formal rationality.

Having established the time for each motion in the process, it becomes possible to set benchmarks. If one operation can be completed in 10 seconds then 6 can be done in a minute, 360 in an hour and 2,880 in an eight-hour shift. And a pay rate for the shift could be set, with a bonus for exceeding it and a pay cut for failing to reach it. Of course, in the beer drinking example, or in an industrial process, you might say that the rate that the operation can be done might decrease over time. But this was no problem for scientific management: it measured, and factored in, fatigue time.

At a stroke, this system solved the soldiering problem by effecting a very fundamental redistribution of power. No longer was it possible for workers to give unrealistic estimates of the time needed to perform a task. How long will it take to drink half a litre of beer? 100 seconds – no more and no less. The manager with the stopwatch now has the power, not the person performing the task.

I have chosen the example of beer drinking as an illustration because we would normally think of something like having a drink as an unregulated activity over which we ourselves have choice, and this was more or less how industrial work was, pre-Taylorism.[8] The impact, or more accurately the intention, of Taylorism and scientific management was to evacuate all discretion from work processes so

---

8   Of course it's relative: there are legal and social controls over drinking, just as there were on work before scientific management.

that the organization would become akin to machines and workers akin to machine parts.

That workers were regarded as no more than components in the organizational machine is important. It reflects very much an engineering mindset, in which the machine was an obvious model and metaphor. It reflects a derogatory attitude towards the supposedly almost less than human Catholics and foreigners that comprised the workforce. But it also reflects a pragmatism: these techniques overcame many of the problems of communication between people who spoke different languages. Perhaps most interesting of all, it reflected a particular kind of ethic, in a way which recalls du Gay's defence of bureaucracy. For Taylor believed that his system embodied an impersonal fairness: the fairness of 'a fair day's wage for a fair day's work'. It is easy to understand how this might be. Workers would no longer be dependant upon the patronage of a work gang leader, but would be paid and worked according to a fixed system. This would be of particular importance to, for example, an immigrant worker from Eastern Europe faced with the established position of an Irish foreman hiring and firing from within his own ethnic group. It is also the case that Taylor's system could make for a safer workplace. At a time when industrial injuries were rife, a system that devised a standard way of working which, if followed, would not just be more productive but would avoid accidents did have an appeal for workers. Taylorism has its problems, as I will explain, but it would be overly facile to dismiss the specifically ethical claims which Taylor made for it.

On the other hand, as one of the most prominent and insightful critics of the Taylorist system, Harry Braverman (1974) points out, for Taylor a fair day's work meant the maximum amount of work a person could physically do without collapsing, and a fair day's pay meant the minimum amount that could be paid to induce the worker to give this level of effort. Braverman remarks that you might just as well say that a fair day's work would be that amount of work which produces an output of equivalent value to what the worker is paid. But if that were so, the process would not yield a profit. Thus, from Braverman's perspective, scientific management must be understood in terms of its value to capitalist profit-seeking and not as any kind of fairness.

The introduction of scientific management provoked an enormous reaction. It is tempting from a current-day perspective to see it as a natural and unremarkable development in industrial organization. Because it, in fact, happened, it's tempting to think it *had* to happen. But that it happened was the outcome of a struggle which at the time did not seem determined, any more than present-day arguments about how to organize have a pre-ordained outcome. Shenhav (1999) shows how scientific management was a part of a whole 'standardization movement' (which included things like the standardization of tool sizes and machine parts) which was bitterly contested. Many critics said that standardization was inimical to American individualism, and would sap innovation and entrepreneurship.

Taylorism, specifically, was extensively resisted by workers and their embryonic trade unions. It is not hard to see why. The system entailed a massive transfer of power from workers to managers. It reduced autonomy, eroded working conditions and threatened unemployment (as more could be done with fewer people). Fundamentally, as Braverman and many others have explained, Taylorism implemented a radical and near complete separation between conception and execution, meaning planning and decision-making, on the one hand, and carrying out orders on the other. This was the division of labour set out in Taylor's principles. Managers would decide, workers would act accordingly. One of the key decisions was over the hiring and training of workers, previously carried out by the work group itself. This is why Taylor's principle included the scientific selection and training of workers. Given all of this, the meaning of Taylor's final principle, co-operation between managers and workers, was a rather truncated one: workers had to undertake to do the work in the prescribed manner in return for the wages on offer (or fines for non-compliance), and leave everything else to the managers.

Everywhere that scientific management was introduced it caused conflict. Workers went on strike or left their jobs, and T&M studies were actually banned in US defence plants. Interestingly, it was not just workers who reacted against Taylorism. Owners and some senior managers objected too. For the system created a new breed of powerful managers, mainly production engineers. If, previously, workers had had the power that came from knowledge of how to do work, now it was these engineers who had privileged access to a baffling array of new knowledge. With their stopwatches, their myriad sheets of benchmarks and pay rates, they presented a threat not just to workers but owners and some managers. Taylor himself was sacked, because his employers did not appreciate the industrial unrest his system engendered. Embittered, he insisted that his ideas had not been properly implemented. But, importantly, he inspired a devoted group of followers who propagated and developed his ideas well into the twentieth century.

If the development of scientific management was contested, the watershed came with the First World War (1914–18). Now there was a patriotic imperative to maximize production of armaments.[9] Workers and others were asked to set aside their reservations in the interests of the war effort and, by and large, they agreed. But once the war was over, these methods were established and maintained. That is not to say that resistance ceased. On the contrary, Taylorist systems continued to provoke a wide array of responses. Sabotage, absenteeism and high staff turnover were the most obvious but, more insidiously, perhaps, was the tendency of such systems to breed low commitment and low quality.

What was going on here was a kind of unintended consequence of a type I indicated earlier. Taylorism treated workers as being motivated in a very simple way – carrot and stick, or pain and pleasure. There were targets: exceed them and gain a bonus, fail to meet them and get a fine. This idea that people are motivated solely by money had a self-fulfilling quality. If money was all that was on offer, then money could be all that mattered. Why should the workers care if what they produced was shoddy, why should they be committed to the product or to the company if they were simply treated as money-motivated robots? They did not. Instead, they churned out their product, got their bonuses (or didn't) and looked elsewhere for the things that made life worthwhile. In some cases, this was no more than the end-of-week drinking session. In others, it took the form of a remarkable flourishing of working-class culture in industrial areas. In Britain, the choirs of South Wales, the brass bands of Yorkshire colliery towns, the art clubs and mechanics institutes of many nineteenth- and twentieth-century towns are just some examples. The activities of trade unions and, later, the Communist Party were more political consequences. Much later, as these areas became de-industrialized, these activities in turn collapsed, which showed that they were indeed a by-product of industrial organization, leaving a cultural vacuum often either left hollow or filled with a diet of drugs, crime and reality-TV.

The evacuation of meaning from work also had implications from a managerial perspective. That so little energy and commitment went into work, that the quality of products was no longer a matter of pride to workers constituted the backdrop to much that was to happen in the management of organizations during the twentieth century and beyond (as I said earlier, yesterday's solutions are often the source of today's problems). But that lesson was a long time in coming, and even then was learnt in ways which reflected the engineering legacy of scientific

9 This was true in the US even before that country's entry into the war in 1917 because US firms were producing arms for the war and there was already a sense that this was a patriotic priority.

management. In the meantime, what actually happened was an intensification of the Taylorist approach with the introduction of a system which, being pioneered at the Ford motor company, carries the unsurprising name of Fordism.

The Fordist system added a crucial innovation to that of Taylorism: the moving assembly line. Here, a mechanically driven conveyor belt brings the work to the worker, who stands at a fixed work station and performs a small operation upon the car (as it was at Ford) before it moves down to the next operative until the finished product emerges at the other end. The moving assembly line entails a massive simplification of the Taylor system because a huge number of those bodily movements which hitherto had to be prescribed by the T&M study were now mechanized. Workers were even more than before rendered as parts within the organizational machine. Moreover, it became possible for managers to gain greater control of the rate of work through the simple expedient of speeding up the conveyor belt.

But at the same time, and it is an important theoretical and practical lesson, this apparent increase in managerial power produced new kinds of power amongst workers (again, an example of an unintended consequence). For now it was possible to bring production to a grinding halt throughout the factory by the simple expedient of stopping production in one place. The familiar phrase 'putting a spanner in the works' captures this. By dropping (as it might be) a spanner in the conveying mechanism, the whole line stopped. And, in fact, this kind of sabotage is an enduring feature of Fordist systems. Ford itself managed to implement the system through a combination of offering relatively high wages and operating, especially during the 1920s and 1930s, in a high unemployment era. Nonetheless, not only sabotage but high levels of absenteeism and staff turnover dogged Fordism in similar ways and for similar reasons to the basic Taylorist system.

conclusion

Fordism represents the fullest working out of a particular, massively influential, approach to organizing work. So significant is it that many commentators have spoken of a Fordist era. As Merkle (1980) explains, it spread to all parts of the industrialized world, and its techniques were by no means confined to capitalist societies. On the contrary, Lenin and Stalin both admired Taylor's work and used precisely his techniques to undertake speedy industrialization of the largely agrarian economy of the Soviet Union after the 1917 Russian revolution. That they did so reminds us that, whatever difficulties it faced or created, this approach to organizing allowed unprecedented levels of productivity. And we shouldn't be too moralistic about this: Soviet industrial productivity created the tanks and planes which played a central part in the defeat of Nazi Germany.

And this of course brings us right back to Weber's ideas. His observation that rational-legal, or bureaucratic, organization was taking over was the observation that such organizations were more technically efficient than others. The modern world is the world of efficiency in which the focus is upon the best means to achieve particular ends. The management principles of Taylor and Ford embody just this formal rationality and continue to define, at least partially and perhaps substantially, management to the present day. For, on the one hand, despite some talk to the contrary, it is possible to find organizations all over the world following precisely these principles in industrial settings which Taylor would have immediately recognized as similar to the steel fields of nineteenth-century America. But, on the other hand, even where the settings are less familiar, the basic idea of a rationality of means as the sole focus of managerial concern, the ideology of formal rationality, if you will, has endured.

Weber and Taylor were, of course, very different creatures. Taylor was an architect of this ideology whereas Weber was an observer and, in significant respects, a critic. They therefore appear in organization theory in rather different ways. In conventional, textbook accounts Taylor is seen as a pioneer in the emergence of modern management. The position of Weber is more interesting. His adoption into the 'canon' of organization theory (as opposed to conventional sociology) relied on a very partial reading of his work that ignored his reservations about bureaucracy and elevated his 'ideal type' to the status of a design model.

In this chapter I have tried to offer a somewhat different overview of these themes to that conventionally presented to students. On the one hand, I have drawn attention to how the ideas of Weber and Taylor inform organization theory, and this in some ways overlaps with conventional accounts. But, on the other hand, I have tried to indicate some difficulties, limitations and complexities which such accounts fail to mention. However, that is not to say that these conventional accounts are unaware or unconcerned with at least some version of the problems I have alluded to. They are, and in the next chapter I turn to that body of organization theory which purports to rectify the limitations of bureaucracy and scientific management.

2

Human Relations Theory and People Management

> *The minutiae of the human soul ... emerged as a new domain for management.*
> *Nikolas Rose*

Conventional textbooks often set up a simple story about organization theory which has a very appealing structure. In this story, there is a good guy and a bad guy. Who gets to play which role sometimes shifts, but most often the bad guy is the scientific management approach and the good guy is human relations theory. This is a flawed story in my view, and the way I will tell the story emphasizes the many connections and similarities between the two. But I suppose the fact that I am referring to 'the two' implies that there must be some points of difference as well. Maybe so, but it is a different sort of difference to that which standard commentaries identify.

Human relations theory (HRT) is normally thought of as having its roots in the Hawthorne Studies conducted in the 1920s and 1930s at the Hawthorne works of the Western Electric Company, near Chicago in the United States. These studies have now taken on an almost mythological status within the study of organization, so that the details of what happened there and even when they happened are reported differently in different accounts. For example, different books give 1923, 1924 and 1927 as the date the studies started. Related to this mythology is a disjuncture between these precise details of what was done and what was written and the received version of what HRT is. Since HRT was the work of many years and many people, it contains a huge amount of variation and nuance (some of it extremely interesting) which is not captured by the received version.[1] Although it would certainly be worthwhile to look at the detail (if you fancy it, Schwartzman, 1993, is a nice place to start), it is perhaps more important to examine the received version, for it is this which figures most strongly both in textbooks and, consequently, in the way that HRT is used to structure understandings of organizations, especially on the part of their managers. Indeed, as Nancy Harding (2003) observes of the conventional canon of management thinkers:

> ... neither the writers themselves nor indeed what they wrote is important. What defines them as important ... is what they signify, i.e. conventionality, continuity, the conservative way, or, in one word, patriarchy. (2003: 117)

The basic suggestion of the received version of HRT is that through a series of experiments and interviews, the Hawthorne researchers and, most notably, the man who became their chief popularizer and canonical emblem, Elton Mayo, identified the importance of 'the human factor' in organizations. That meant that workers were now recognized as having social needs and interests such that they could no longer be regarded as the economically motivated automatons envisaged by Taylorism.

Within these terms, two parts of the studies stand out as being especially important: the 'illumination experiment' and the 'bank wiring room experiment'. In the first of these, lighting levels were varied up and down within an experimental group of workers, whilst light levels were left unchanged within a control group. Almost all of the lighting changes led to an increase in productivity and, most interesting of all, productivity also increased within the control group. What was going on? Apparently, it was the fact that something 'unusual' was happening and that the workers felt that they were part of it and that what they were doing was of interest and importance

---

1 This same disjuncture is present in relation to Taylor's work (and scholarly commentaries on it) and that of many other organizational theorists. It isn't a matter of saying that the received version is deficient in detail or scholarship. They are different things for different purposes. Apart from anything else, received versions are simpler and more memorable. In many ways my purpose in this book is to put out another version of organization theory, no more scholarly than the received version but hopefully no less memorable.

to the researchers. It was this that caused the increase in productivity and which demonstrated that the workers could not be regarded as mere parts in the organizational machine. Thus was born the notion of the 'Hawthorne effect', a staple part not just of organization theory but of social science as a whole.

The other study I want to mention is that conducted in the bank wiring room. Here, a small group of male workers were engaged in producing electrical components. It emerged that the group set informal norms around production levels so that, rather than produce their maximum output (which would earn them a bonus), the workers performed sub-optimally. These norms were enforced by a mixture of peer pressure (including physical sanction) and an unofficial 'gang leader'. This suggested that workers were not solely motivated by economic considerations and, moreover, that the 'informal side of the organization' was as important as, or maybe even more important than, the formal side (i.e. the rules and official hierarchy).

The discovery of the human factor, so the story goes, ushered in a new era in which workers' needs were acknowledged and met. This claim fits not just the 'good guy, bad guy' story, it also promotes a version of organization theory as gradually discovering and refining truths, much in the way that science is supposed to proceed. There is one tiny flaw in all this, however: it's not true. It's not true for lots of reasons. One is that an interest in workers going beyond economic concerns can be found well before Hawthorne. It was present in the various attempts by nineteenth-century industrialists, especially those of Quaker background, to meet the 'moral needs' of workers. This is evidenced by towns like Port Sunlight and Bourneville in the UK, where housing and religious and communal activities were designed to cater for workers' leisure time and to provide an environment conducive to good living. True, it was the new 'science' of psychology rather than paternalistic religiosity that informed HRT but they share a similar humanizing imperative, and the latter had a paternalism of its own.

The second issue is that the original impetus for the Hawthorne experiments was firmly located within the tradition of scientific management, well established by the 1920s. The desire to ascertain the effect of lighting levels on productivity was informed by the idea that management was about the control of physical variables, and in fact there were many other experiments designed to explore a whole array of such variables.

Finally, and crucially, it is simply wrong to think that Taylor had been unaware of, or was uninterested in, the informal side of the organization. On the contrary, the heart of Taylor's project was an attempt to overcome its effects. For the output restrictions observed in the Bank Wiring Room were nothing other than an instance of what Taylor has identified as the systematic soldiering of the workforce. That is not to say that his approach was the same as HRT; it was not. For whereas Taylor sought to eradicate the informal side of the organization, the human relations message was to acknowledge its irrepressibility and to find ways of managing it into an alignment with the formal parts and purposes of the organization.

And so now HRT begins to take on a very different aspect. In one way it is a response to the failure, or at least limitations, of scientific management as a means of organizational control. But it is a response which in many ways offers not an alternative to, but an extension of, scientific management. What I mean to say is that HRT bears the same footprint of formal or instrumental rationality as that which is to be found in scientific management. My former colleague John Roberts wrote a highly illuminating case study around this theme some years ago (Roberts, 1984). He contrasts the approaches of 'Dave' and 'Val' to managing their teams of telesales workers. Dave is a scientific management type of manager, who tries to avoid any human contact with his staff and treats them as economically motivated automatons. Val takes a more human relations type of approach. She tries to understand the problems and anxieties of her staff and to encourage their wider motivations to work. But – and this is the crucial point – they both sought to control their teams: one by *avoiding* human relationships and one *through* human relationships.

If this is right, then the difference between scientific management and HRT is a 'tactical' one. That's a real difference, and it would be crass to deny it, not least because the two tactics create different working environments which will be experienced as such by people within them. But it would also be crass to romanticize that difference. For how will Dave and Val be judged, by others and, perhaps, themselves? According to the extent to which their approaches yield higher or lower sales. This is why they are both instrumentally rational versions of organization.

Why, then, does the received version of HRT fight shy of acknowledging its commonality with scientific management? I think there are two reasons for this. One is straightforward and relates to some specific difficulties faced by management as an occupation or even, aspirationally, a profession. The other is much more complicated and is to do with the idea of 'humanism'.

Later in this chapter I will talk quite a bit about management as an occupation. But what I want to say here is that the establishment of it as a respectable, let alone respected, occupation was by no means straightforward. Today, we live in a world where to be a manager is, in many people's eyes, to be recognized as a person of some consequence (though this may be changing, as I will discuss in Chapter 5). But this was not always so. In the early nineteenth century, the term 'manager' was regarded with some suspicion, much as we might use the word 'cowboy' today. As I mentioned in the last chapter, the new breed of scientific managers was also accused of undermining individual initiative and freedom. By the twentieth century, managers were much better established, but the legacy of scientific management with its conflicts and inhumane efficiency hardly made it a prestigious label. Satirized and derided in films like Charlie Chaplin's *Modern Times* and novels like Aldous Huxley's *Brave New World*, management had an image problem in the 1920s and 1930s. It's not hard to see why. Imagine a manager going home and being questioned by his (for most managers of the day were men) child:

Child: What do you do all day, Dad?
Dad: Well, I, sort of, exploit people.
Child: How do you mean?
Dad: Well, you know, I dehumanize them by making them work as hard as I can for as little money as possible.
Child: Oh.

It was embarrassing stuff. A much better picture was offered by HRT. Management could now be reconfigured as an altogether more humane undertaking which ameliorated rather than inflamed social conflict and, perhaps most important of all, was about 'helping' rather than exploiting the worker. This latter point came out of the tendency of Mayo, in particular, to conceptualize worker resistance as a psychological maladjustment rather than a rational response to conditions of employment. Famously, or infamously, Mayo went so far as to propose that membership of a trade union was a sign of mental illness. In fact, in this respect, Taylor's writings show much more empathy with workers' experiences than those of Mayo. Taylor after all had worked as a machine operator, and he did not find worker recalcitrance particularly objectionable at a personal level, albeit that he wanted to overcome it. But that overcoming presented management as, nakedly, being about power. Mayo's less sympathetic account of worker resistance paradoxically cast the manager as assisting the worker to make a normal adjustment to factory life.

So now a different conversation becomes possible:

Child: What do you do all day, Dad?
Dad: Well, I, sort of, help people.
Child: How do you mean?
Dad: Well, you know, if they feel unhappy at work I make them see that I care about them and that it's not so bad.
Child: Oh, Dad. That's great.

We probably shouldn't discount the fact that being able to give a positive sounding account of one's work to family and friends might persuade managers to embrace HRT. But, in any case, there were wider constituencies to whom, in a less naïve way, a similar account could helpfully be given. In a society[2] racked by social and industrial conflict, and extremely fearful that such conflict might lead to an emulation of the 1917 Russian Revolution, managers really needed to present a more humane and less confrontational face than they had hitherto been able to do. And there was more at stake here than the manipulation of image. It was also the case that the scientific management system had indeed thrown up new problems – sabotage, poor quality, high staff turnover, absenteeism – to which the human relations approach might offer a solution. 'Technical' and 'ideological' factors are never separable: they reinforce each other.

All of this is fairly easy to understand. What is perhaps less clear is the more general question of the place of humanism within western societies, of which HRT management is but one, specific, manifestation. There is so much that could be said about this that I hesitate to plunge in, but it is necessary for me to do so because it is not possible to understand organization without seeing how it stands in this wider context.[3]

---

2 I mean Britain, the US and other industrialized countries between the two World Wars.

3 In the pages which follow I am glossing a fairly freeform version of 'post-structuralism'. It would disrupt my purposes to elaborate this but see, for example, Burrell (1988), Rose (1989) and Hacking (1991) for some of the work which has informed my account.

⬤⬤⬤ what is it to be human?

Part of what has made modern societies modern is a move away from traditional belief systems in which the social order was simply pre-ordained by the will of God. The eighteenth-century Enlightenment had broken down much of this reasoning – for example, the belief that kings ruled by divine right – and, as mentioned in the last chapter, had substituted the idea that individuals could use their own reason rather than rely upon the received authority of others. Clearly Weber's charting of the rise of rational-legal, as against traditional, authority and of the development of the bureaucratic organization, was part of the same flow of thought. But if individuals, rather than God or his representatives in the Church or the Monarchy, were now at the centre of things – who were these individuals? There were many takes on this question, but they crystallized around the idea of autonomous human beings, complete and sufficient in themselves, capable of rationality, capable of choice, capable of moral conduct and, by virtue of all possessing these traits, all entitled to certain rights.

So we find, from the Enlightenment onwards, the understanding that people had the right to be treated in certain ways. This led to all kinds of reforms, including the ideas that people could (with certain restrictions such as, until the twentieth century, being male) have a say in who governed them; have a fair trial; speak their opinions without punishment; own their own property; be equal in the eyes of the law and so on. These are all very familiar things. It is easy to see how central such ideas are to modern forms of organization. When we think of a worker agreeing to work in exchange for a certain sum of money, we are pre-supposing a whole series of choices and rights. It is a bizarre thought that, for someone of my age, some didn't always apply to my grandmother and almost none to my great-great-great grandfather. This should alert us to the historical mutability of the idea of 'personhood' – or, what a human being is. Who knows what it will mean for our great-great-great grandchildren, or even for our children?[4]

This idea of personhood substantially deepened in the twentieth century. It moved from a philosophical, political or legal notion to a much more embodied or personalized one. If eighteenth and

---

4   Consider, for example, the possible impact of developments in genetic science and technology for how we come to conceive of personhood in the future.

nineteenth centuries had established some ideas about economic and political personhood (or at least, as I have suggested, manhood), then the twentieth century extended this into the psychological sphere. The intellectual revolution associated with Freud (but, as with Taylor, no less attributable to others) established human beings as no mere conscious decision-making machines but as possessors of an unconscious and of all of the complexities of neurosis, motivation, desire and so on that map us out as human in our present-day understanding of that term. The 'I' had been given depth, so that we learned to understand our real selves as a complex, multi-layered thing, understandable only partially to ourselves but perhaps accessible through the expertise of a psychoanalyst. 'Subconsciously,' someone might say, 'I think that what attracted me to my husband was the way he's an authority figure, a bit like my father.' It is a surprising thought that almost no normal person would have said such a thing, or have been understood if they had said it, as little as 120 years ago.

And, of course, at the same time that all this was going on, there was also a steady but sure erosion of the religious belief which had been the dominant way of understanding the self and its relationship with the wider world for several centuries, in its Christian form, and perhaps for all of history in one form or another. To be sure that change has happened slowly and, for a great many people, not at all. But, where it did, it placed the individual at the centre of the universe. It suggested that people – and perhaps society – were not just important but that they were all that there was. Life ended with death, and the authority of God was replaced either by the authority of society, most likely in the form of the State, or by no more than the individual pursuit of desire and pleasure.

It is easy to see that all of the main currents of western society in, say, the last century have been concerned in making sense of this: Fascism, Communism, Existentialism, Hippie Culture, Neo-liberalism and our present culture of individualistic consumption of material goods are all examples.

Did any of this add up to a better, more accurate picture of personhood or the relation of people one to another? That really seems like an impossible question to answer. I suppose that from a religious perspective there would be some answers (mainly negative), but then adherence to a religion might be seen as no more than a dogmatic response to the very question posed by the dissolution of certainty. I think that since the picture we currently have of personhood is so very different to that held even a relatively short time ago, then it is likely that the future will have a different picture and that therefore it would be foolish to give undue weight to our present picture. What is certain is that modern understandings of the human being have had dramatic effects upon how we live, upon art, culture, politics – upon everything that human beings do.

And that, of course, includes organizations. How could it not? The puzzling thing is that these kinds of themes and discussions are so absent from most of the organization theory textbooks. How can it be that they just assume that the way things are round about now is some kind of immutable, stable truth?[5] I suspect that most organization theorists would say that all the themes I have alluded to (in the most cursory way) are about 'something else' – politics, philosophy, society – but that is manifestly nonsense. How could organizations possibly be abstracted from these?

Returning to HRT, it seems clear to me that its appeal, its very emergence, fitted into this shifting understanding of personhood like, to use a clichéd term, a hand in a glove. The invocation of 'humanity' is one obvious clue to this. For HRT engaged directly with emerging understandings about the 'depth' of personhood. It suggested that 'beneath' the economic motivations of Taylorist workers lay some more profound realities, realities which it took a very specialized kind of manager to understand (another reason why we should give managers respect, then). But understanding was only one part of the picture. Much more important, as for the psychoanalysts, was 'adjustment'. The new domain of the psyche was also a domain in which problems occurred and had to be dealt with. The self was no longer something just to be taken at face value, but was a terrain of worry.

That worry was both social – the problems of criminality, madness, delinquency, alcoholism, perversion and so on – and individual. Individuals, along with their autonomy, their rights, their choices, had acquired responsibilities and anxieties. Freedom, in Erich Fromm's haunting (1942) phrase, had brought the 'fear of freedom'. You can see exactly the same thing today, in very advanced form. On the one hand, there is an ever greater array of social worries about what people do with their freedom – molest children, plant

---

5   This is particularly weird given the way that most current texts emphasize how rapid is 'change' in organizations and their world. But change in that kind of thought is only considered in the most limited of ways. See Chapter 4.

bombs, take drugs. On the other hand, there is huge individual insecurity – am I earning enough, good in bed, living a healthy
lifestyle? Am I too fat, too much in debt, gettting good enough
grades?

All this is to say that a new terrain opened up, in organizations at
least as much as elsewhere, into which management could now be
inserted. This, I think, is the real significance of the Hawthorne
Studies. They legitimated a new managerial arena. At one level it could
be read as an imposition. Management was no longer concerned with
what workers did – with, if you will, the body – but with what people
are. Worker hopes, fears, motivations, anxieties, aspirations all fell
into the locus of management. One reading of this would be to see
organizations as becoming ever more intrusive. The private, non-work
sphere gets progressively more eroded. For these new understandings
of work began to break down the dividing line between work and the
real, true self. I mean: under scientific management systems it might be
possible to say that your real self was what lay outside work: your
family, the pub, whatever. But HRT begins (although less dramatically
than some of its successors) to say that that distinction is false.

However, if my earlier idea about the changing nature of personhood is correct, then it follows that neither the claim that the real self
lies outside of work nor the claim that it lies inside of work can be
sustained. All we can say is that, at various times, different apprehensions of personhood hold good. So isn't it more to the point to say not
that HRT invaded the territory of the private self but that it actually
contributed to mapping the territory out as one to be either left alone
or invaded? For it tells us that the human being is always, unavoidably,
present at work. This has profound consequences for organizations,
but it is also highly significant for individuals. For if modernity left a
pervasive void of meaning and a pervasive insecurity about identity,
then work now stood ready to provide meaning and identity. After all,
what is one of the first things we say when we meet a new person? We
might start by asking their name, and then, perhaps, where they come
from. But very soon we will ask: what do you do?

Once work begins to express and define who we are (and in the
process of doing so, to close certain things down as to what we are
not), a whole new set of concerns becomes manifest in organizations.
Once HRT had entered the world of organizations and organization
theorists, a whole edifice of knowledge about people at work was
gradually elaborated. Such knowledge is the staple of the conventional study of organizations and includes such things as personality

type, motivation and job satisfaction, group dynamics, leadership and much more. It is tempting to see these as more or less descriptive accounts of people at work, but this is wrong for two reasons. The first is an extension of what I have already tried to say. There is no ultimate description of people but rather ascriptions which, if believed and enforced, are taken as descriptions – they constitute or construct reality. For example, is the difference between a child and an adult a real difference, or is it rather that where we draw the line and enforce it (for example, by conferring certain rights at particular ages) takes on the appearance of a real difference? We could say that people divide into those who are right-handed and those who are left-handed and confer different rights to them, but we don't. On the other hand, we can and do say that people divide into male and female and, in many societies, confer different rights accordingly. Or we divide people into different nationalities and confer different rights accordingly. These things are a matter of what is socially agreed and also of power – who has the power to draw the distinctions and to enforce the effects of these distinctions.

So when personality types are divided into, say, introvert and extrovert, or any of the many other variations on this theme in organization theory, and when on the basis of this ascription decisions are made about who to employ and who not to employ, then exactly the same processes of distinction making and enforcement are present. The legacy of HRT has been to multiply these schema for making distinctions between people, and you can see in any organization theory textbook an endless array of models, typologies, 2-by-2 matrices and so on which replicate these distinctions but treat them as descriptions rather than ascriptions – as being rooted in a self-evident truth rather than being the outcome of a social process. In this way, organization theory is a part of making this social process happen. So, to take some well-known examples: the distinctions Maslow draws between different motivators; or Herzberg's distinction of motivators and hygiene factors; or the distinction of task and role orientation in management style; or McGregor's theory X and theory Y – all these serve to constitute or construct the organizational world and do not simply describe it.

Now, undoubtedly, the drawing of distinctions is almost unavoidable if we are to make any kind of sense of the world around us, including that of organizations (even to speak of 'the world around us' is to make a distinction). And it is not the case that this began in organization theory with HRT. After all, scientific management draws all kinds of distinctions between efficiency and inefficiency, for example. However, because HRT draws the 'whole person' into the organizational ambit, the impact of all of these supposedly descriptive distinctions is potentially much greater. The stakes are very high when we think about organizations, just because work is so central a part of society; but the stakes get even higher when work organizations and personhood become inextricably linked. And this means that those of us who study organizations, and the much larger number of us who work in them, need to be much more sceptical than organization theory normally encourages us to be.

The constitutive or constructive nature of organization theory is one reason why we have to be cautious about the way we use its concepts to think about people in organizations. But there is a second issue, and this relates to the continuities between HRT and scientific management which I pointed to earlier. For not only does organization theory contribute to constituting what it claims to be describing but it does so in particular ways, for particular reasons. The impetus for HRT was that of organizational control and, more particularly, the attempt by managers to gain control over organizational processes. So the kind of knowledge produced and the uses to which it is put have to be read in the light of that aspiration for control. Organization theory is often, and certainly in the case of HRT, indistinguishable from theories of managing. Organization theorists have often been, to use Baritz's evocative (1960) phrase, 'servants of power'. That may or may not be a good thing (I think it is a bad thing), but it must mean that organization theory has to be read with an eye to the purposes it serves, which means giving more attention to management than I have so far done.

the rise and rise of management

Management has been one of the great success stories of the modern world. As many writers have remarked – so many that it has almost become clichéd – the etymological origins of management lie in two terms – the French *menager* and the Italian *maneggiare* – the first denoting domestic or household organization, the second the handling of horses. The ultimate origin lies in the Latin word *manus* or hand. What this may be taken to point to (if you will forgive the pun) is the essentially humble and mundane meaning of management, the sense that it is something dispersed, done by everyone. This sense is recalled when we say something like 'I managed to catch the bus on time' or 'I managed to avoid arguing with him'.

But although we do use the word manage in that way, that isn't what we usually think of when we talk about management, and it certainly isn't the kind of thing with which 'management schools' and management studies are normally concerned. They configure management in an altogether more grandiose way. But what is management? There is no straightforward answer to that question, and the problem is not one of definition. It is not that there is some 'thing' – management – to be described and, in being described, delineated from all sorts of other 'things'. As with personhood, what is at stake is a social construction in which competing claims are made about management and, at different times and by different audiences, are accepted. A good illustration of this is found in a study of management which has received far less attention than it deserves:

> I was styled a 'manager' and my wife … was a 'housewife'. I can remember well the blessed relief of leaving my house and its attendant chaos each morning to go off to my oh-so-demanding 'management' job. In what sense … was my wife not 'managing' and in what sense was my work … more essentially *managerial* than hers? At work I had another woman to make sure I managed properly … This one wasn't styled a manager either, but the same essential question held good for her; in what sense is the work of a secretary *not* managerial? (Mant, 1977: 1)

I think that Mant's questions in this passage do two things. One is to remind us that management carries the embedded meaning of the daily accomplishment of life's 'business'. The other is that the way the line gets drawn between managers and others is an accomplishment of power. Some kinds of claims to be a manager don't register, and if they are demanded the response is: 'yeah, of course'. Other kinds of claims jar, and invite the response: 'oh yeah?'. So it's really no great surprise that the two people Mant identifies as being engaged in managerial roles without being awarded the title of manager are women – his wife and his secretary. *Their* kind of management is just boring old house management ('oh yeah?'). *Real* management is what the guys do, with spreadsheets and strategies and meetings and budgets. It's what managers do ('yeah, of course').

So, sometimes, management seems to mean a group of people – managers. In this way we may talk about 'the management', and mean, usually, a group distinct from 'the workers'. What makes them managers? Well, one important answer might be just that they are called managers. I'll come back to this, but one thing which is notable about present day organizations is how the title of manager has become something of a debased currency, so that what was once a loo cleaner might now be glossed as a facilities inspection and hygiene manager. This is interesting – on a fairly lax interpretation of the term interesting – because it points to the mutability of the status of managers. Over the last one hundred years or more, and especially in the last few decades, we've got used to the idea of managers being fairly high status, a desirable career option, respected and well-paid. But as I mentioned earlier, this wasn't always the case, and perhaps is ceasing to be so, as discussed in Chapter 5, so management had to go through a long process of what would nowadays be called 'image-building'. That process was ultimately successful, though:

> Management will remain a basic and dominant institution perhaps as long as Western Civilization itself survives. (Drucker, 1955: 1)

This is heady stuff. To go from horse-handling to bulwark of civilization is no mean achievement and if the tone of Drucker's eulogy is rather breathless, it does no more than sum up what many others said and believed. Note that he is not talking about managers per se, but about management as an 'institution'. No doubt there is some overlap between the two, but the point is that it renders management as something more than 'the management'. How did management achieve this position? Analysts are divided between at least three competing explanations, which I have outlined elsewhere (Grey, 1999). First, there is a 'technical' explanation – that management arose to solve the functional problems of large-scale organization. Second, there is an 'elite' explanation – that management arose to define and defend the interests of a particular group, namely managers. Third, there is a 'political' explanation – that management arose in order to control and discipline workers.

Earlier I talked about the struggles that management engaged in to make itself legitimate in the eyes of society. These took two forms, of which one was a kind of technical justification – that management made things more efficient; and the other a more ideological justification – that management helped to make things more humane. Of course these are not really separate so much as reinforcing justifications: scientific management had as part of its pitch a fair division of labour and a fair reward, whilst human relations approaches have always claimed, even if they have been unable to prove it, that workers who are managed humanely are also more productive. In this sense, HRT is about humanization as technique.

Looked at in this way, it is easy to see the relationship between technical and elite views of management. If management is a technical necessity, arising from the functional requirements for efficiency in large-scale enterprises, then this makes out a strong case for the elite status of managers. A much stronger case than, for example, a bald demand for status, power and money. That may be what drives the elite explanation, but for it to work it has to be translated into terms with a greater legitimacy, and the two-pronged claims (technical and ideological) within the case for management do just that.

Of course, someone might object to this by saying that what is important is that it is true that management fulfils a technical necessity, and because it is true then managers came to form an elite group. All my talk of legitimation is beside the point. Against this, I could point to the argument that management is really about control, not technical necessity. My imaginary heckler might then say that this too misses the point since it is precisely the delivery of control – whether delivered through hard systems or soft soap – which constitutes the technical necessity of management. But now I have a good put-down line, which is that it is highly questionable whether management does in fact deliver such control, even accepting that this is its aim, because of the issues of resistance and unintended consequences I rehearsed in the first chapter; the idea that management is a perennially failing operation. And if my 'theoretical' arguments on this aren't acceptable, then just consider the fact that, despite well over a century of trying to find the answers to managerial problems, it remains the case that organizations are continually chasing new solutions and new approaches – and the job of management appears never to be done.

So, at the very least, the truth of the technical necessity for management is endlessly debatable and requires the continual advancement of claims which may or may not be accepted by particular people at particular times. It is therefore quite sensible to look at the way those claims are advanced. And here I think we have to go into deeper water than simply talking about their content towards considering what it is that makes them, at least potentially, plausible.

management and modernism

It is no coincidence that Peter Drucker talked about management's dominance in the context of western civilization. Earlier I talked about modern understandings of personhood and the way that the breakdown of religious belief brought with it a new accent upon the individual. But alongside and in various ways linked to that came another development. If the world and what happened in it was no longer thought of in terms of the will and design of God, it became possible to think of that world instead as something that could be ordered according to the will and design of people. Social organization ceases to be pre-ordained but becomes an arena for intervention and control.

Control is perhaps a key term here. The emergence of experimental natural science and the growing body of theory that went with it, which quickened from the seventeenth century onwards, yielded the possibility of control over the physical circumstances of life. In its wake came a huge array of new technologies – from medicine to energy generation – which fundamentally altered the relationship between human beings and nature. But if the physical world could be controlled in this way, then why should social organization be any different? It is from this basic question that, amongst other things, the positivism I discussed in the Introduction emerged. For at heart, positivism is the attempt to apply the same reasoning to social phenomena as had been introduced to the physical realm.

Obviously the attempt to control social organization was not confined to the modern world that emerged from the scientific revolution. Rulers of all kinds have always sought, and often achieved, control over people, territories, money and so on. What was different, though, was the idea that this could be done systematically through the development and application of the new bodies of knowledge which emerge in the modern era – statistics, economics and sociology being some of the more obvious examples. To design society as if it were a machine, running according to rules which were fully understood and demonstrated – that was the dream. And it is easy to see that this dovetails with Weber's observations about the rise of the bureaucratic organization, for what was this other than a rule-based social machine?

It should not be thought that this search for control was animated solely by a drive for power, and again in this way it perhaps differs from other, pre-modern attempts at control. For along with the search for control was a strong ideology of progress. Just as the natural world could be controlled for the better, for a healthier, more comfortable and richer life, so social life could be controlled in order to yield improvements. Society could become more educated, more knowledgeable, more civilized and cultured (even 'society' conceived of as an object of analysis and a defined arena of behaviour is part of this modern revolution). This of course did require control, for it meant purging ignorance and bad behaviour. Perhaps this too could be thought of as an intervention in nature. Human beings might be naturally corrupt and vicious, just as mountains were naturally difficult to cross. But if you could build roads to cross mountains, then why couldn't you build institutions to improve humanity?

Management is interesting to me because it precisely traverses these twin tracks of modern thought – the systematic control of nature and the systematic control of society. For if the revolution in natural science made possible the steam engines and precision engineering of the factory, then the revolution in social science lent itself to attempts to control the factory workers. Or, to put it differently and perhaps rather better, there is no sharp distinction to be drawn in the modern world between the natural and social domains. Both, as Ian Hacking (1983) has it, become arenas which can be 'represented' and 'intervened' in. What that distinction points to goes beyond what I have said so far, and is worth pausing to consider.

At one level, and I think it is the one that we normally think of, when we think of such things at all, the modern world represents no more than the discovery of ways of intervening. That is, the dumb world was just sitting there, ready and waiting to have things done to it once people got round to working out how to do them. When they did, modernity got going. But this misses a crucial part of what happened. Before intervention could really begin there needed to be a new way of thinking about, and knowing, the world – a way of representing it. That wasn't about discovering new things, so much as 're-presenting' old things in a new way. Was poverty part of the ordained world of God? Or was it because poor people were lazy? Or was it because rich people had grabbed all the wealth? Represent it the first way and intervention is at best pointless and at worse sinful. Represent it in one of the other ways, and intervention becomes possible. More than that, it calls forth a multiplication of representations, for example, drawing the boundary between rich and poor and collecting statistics on how many people are poor, where they live and how they live. So now representation is both a new way of thinking and a new way of knowing. And it is a 'problem' to be dealt with or intervened in – perhaps by punishing the poor for their laziness, perhaps by castigating the rich for their greed, depending upon how the representation was effected.

A similar example, which I talked about earlier, is the constitutive role of organization theory with its distinctions and categories. But now I am talking about something more fundamental than organization theory: the very basic parameters of how modern views of the world operate. Now it is of course the case that this can be discussed in much more sophisticated ways than I have done here, and a host of social theorists and philosophers have done just that, but I am not going to do so. One reason is just my own ignorance. But this necessity can become a virtue for the following reason. The camp followers of modernity, which includes most of the readers of this book as well as myself, don't operate with any very sophisticated grasp of their world, any more than medieval peasants were any great shakes at theology. But a received wisdom, a folk-wisdom, almost, informs our thoughts and actions and, in particular, it informs the theory and practice of management. My concern is to show that this received wisdom is not just 'the way things are' but that it marks management as being embedded in a particular, historically bounded and philosophically informed, view of the world; the details of that history and philosophy I leave to those who are better qualified to discuss it.

For it must be obvious that management is all of a piece with this representation and intervention which I have talked about. At the most basic level, management assumes manageability – that the world can be known and operated upon, and these terms are virtually interchangeable with representation and intervention. In this sense management is something which literally could not have existed, and does not exist, outside of modernity. But, beyond that, management consists of a distinctive series of often extremely complex ways of effecting representations and conducting interventions. For example, consider a workshop in which ten people are making, I don't know, tables. How can it be represented?

We could make a literal representation by drawing a picture, but that wouldn't be a distinctive 'management' representation because it wouldn't (or at least not obviously) allow any kind of managerial intervention. However, if we represented it as a series of inputs and outputs; or an array of costs and incomes; or as a series of bundles of wants and needs (of customers, workers, etc.), then this would be a management representation. It might take the form of a flow chart, a set of accounts or a treatise on marketing or personnel psychology. These are all management representations and they all allow managerial interventions, such as redesign of resource flows; cutting of costs; advertising campaigns to customers or motivation programmes for workers.

So, now, let's go back to managers. If I am right (something which can no means be taken for granted), then there is something more fundamental at stake than the technical, elite and political explanations for its emergence and functioning, even though it has a bearing upon these explanations. Managers are bearers of a particular kind of expertise – the capacity to represent and intervene in particular ways. But these ways are arbitrary and they are contested. They are arbitrary because it is impossible to say that representing the workshop as a balance sheet is more true to reality than painting the scene on a canvas. And because they are arbitrary they must be contestable, in the sense that it is always possible to say that a different representation should be made. This contestability is evident both within management (for example, between an accounting or a human psychology representation) and from without. For, apart from the possibility of representing the workshop in different managerial ways, it is also possible to represent it as, say, a place of exploitation, power and conflict.

I'm going to bring back my imaginary heckler, who might say that I have done no more than state – at excruciating length and in pompous ways – that management is what managers do. Well, maybe that's a fair comment, but I think I've done something a bit more than that. One thing is that I've hopefully shown at a fundamental level what it is that managers do when they manage. That might (perhaps) be interesting in itself, but it also helps to explain the way that these managers are hostages or, if you prefer, emblems of a particular way of looking at the world; itself no more valid and no more enduring than any other. As the Peter Drucker quote suggests, by the middle of the twentieth century, this way of looking at the world was very much in the ascendant. That this was so was in no small part due to the combination of HRT with its supposed opposite in bureaucratic and scientific management approaches to organizations. For taken together these provided the technical and ideological justification for the managerial way of representing and intervening in the realm of organizations.

By welding these things together, it is possible to see how the rise of management is inseparable from the rise of *people* management, or to use what for many years was the preferred term 'man' manage-ment,[6] which grew out of HRT. It is emphatically not the case that other kinds of management (for example, scientific management) were unconcerned with such people management and, indeed, it is impossi-ble to see how it could be. But HRT filled out and made explicit just how extensive was the ambit of management in the modern world. It is no coincidence that the commonest definition of management is given in terms of 'getting things done through other people'. It is a revealing definition in the central role it places on people in manage-ment, the instrumentality of the way it apprehends people and its scope. For what are the 'things' that can be got done in this way? Why, any-thing and everything.

conclusion

The classical issues in the study of organizations with which the first two chapters of this book have been concerned both reflected and contributed to building a powerful and influential edifice. This edifice presents it as self-evident that we live in an organizational world – and moreover, an organizational world of a particular, managerial sort. The significance of this is not, primarily, the rise of an elite group of managers but rather the rise of a managerial apprehension of the orga-nizational world. I stress this because such a view is relatively detached from the fate of managers as an occupational group. As I will explore in later chapters, an increasing accent upon self-management relies upon this managerial apprehension even when it also threatens the position of managers as such.

It is normal when studying organizations as part of a management degree to understand things like bureaucratic theory, scientific man-agement, HRT and management generally as entirely unproblematic. They may sometimes be presented as dated (albeit foundational), but

6 This usage now seems quaint but is by no means an historical curio. For one of the pervasive biases of organization theory, both mainstream and critical, has been to assume that male experience encapsulates experience in general and that 'man' is equivalent to 'human'. This is a very particular, and particularly important, instance of what I was talking about earlier in terms of the construction of mean-ing about what it is to be human: specifically, a gendered construction. See Harding (2003).

to do so does not challenge the way that they take the managerial representation of the organizational world as if it is the only representation (as if, in fact, it is simply reality). The account I have offered is rather different. I suggest that the orthodox story is a construction which conveniently excludes almost everything of importance. First and foremost, it excludes the way that it *is* a construction. Related to that, it also fails to understand how organization theory is part and parcel of a particular philosophical and historical context. And related to *this*, it fails to acknowledge the ways that organization theory provides a technical and ideological legitimation of management, rather than simply the analysis of organizational life it purports to be. Finally, by a relentless focus on a one-sided picture of instrumental rationality and control – whether overtly or, as with human relations approaches, covertly – it fails to understand the severe limitations, both in principle and practice, of this picture.

Defective as this picture may be, it is the one that has been taken forward into the contemporary approaches to studying organizations with which the next three chapters of this book are concerned. The entire tenor of the human relations approach is bound up with the idea of people management. So much so that nowadays management courses virtually always fall into three kinds of components. One is concerned with, precisely, people and is found in modules on organizations, human resource management or some variant of these. Another is concerned with management 'science' – operations, technology and so on. A third straddles the first two, for example, strategy or marketing. The second kind of module addresses 'people' by ignoring them in favour of some fantasy about organizations in which human beings are just removed. The third kind of module usually adopts some quasi-economic model of people as, for example, rational consumers. The first, which is what I am trying to talk about, treats human beings as a recalcitrant but potentially manageable resource – the 'human resource' as we say nowadays. The fact that to do so entails both an impoverished view of people and an at best optimistic and at worse immoral view of management has hardly dented the enthusiasm with which 'people management' has come to occupy a central place in the contemporary study, and practice, of organizations.

3

Organizational Culture and
Self-Management

It's often safer to be in chains than to be free.
Franz Kafka

In 1982, my main preoccupation was with my first 'serious' girlfriend and, when that preoccupation allowed, with attempts to prepare for my forthcoming A-level exams. I hope that this background will both explain and forgive the fact that I was at the time completely unaware of what I consider to be a truly awful book that was published that year. With intellectual roots which recognizably went back to human relations theory (HRT), it was to transform, or rather to symbolize the transformation of organizations for at least the next two decades. The book, which I think still remains the bestselling management book of all time, was *In Search of Excellence* (Peters and Waterman, 1982).

If it was so awful – trite, bombastic, sloppily researched – how come it was so influential? There are many answers to that but perhaps the most obvious is that, like scientific management and human relations, it chimed with the context of its times. North America had, since the end of the war, been the dominant industrial economy in the world but by the late 1970s had come increasingly under threat, especially from competition from Japan in industries like car and consumer goods manufacture, as well as from other emergent 'tiger economies' in South-east Asia. Indeed, a book by colleagues of Peters and Waterman at the management consultants McKinsey & Co, published that same year, had proclaimed the need for US companies to embrace the 'art of Japanese management' (Pascale and Athos, 1982).

Pascale and Athos proposed that American management had been preoccupied with the rational and systemic aspects of management, like organizational structures and strategies. Japanese companies, they said, had a more holistic approach which included attention to soft and irrational factors – people's skills and management styles. Above all, they said, the Japanese focussed on the generation of 'shared values'. Shared values meant that everyone in the organization was committed to common goals such as high-quality output and customer service. As a result, there was less internal conflict, more efficient and effective production and a high degree of motivation and commitment from everyone in the workplace.[1]

It was very much these kinds of shared values which Peters and Waterman identified as being the culture of excellence which obtained within some of America's top performing companies. The way forward, then, was for all companies to develop a set of shared values – a strong, or homogeneous, culture – which would then ensure success. And the news was even better. Because values were shared, organizations no longer needed to maintain large hierarchies of managers overseeing the workforce and enforcing the complicated rules of bureaucracy. The workforce would be empowered and, because of its commitment to the culture of excellence, would use their power wisely and for the benefit of the organization. So it would be possible to massively reduce the number of managerial employees and save a great deal of money as a result.

So you could have better products, less waste, less conflict, better service, a happier and fairer workplace and save money into the bargain – if you could just get the culture right. Unfortunately it proved to be a big 'if'. This confident, even utopian, vision of the future has the appearance of optimism, but it was bred of something less cheerful. Apart from increased competition from Asia, the US continued to bear the scars of the Vietnam and Cambodia wars and to suffer from the effects of the oil price rises of the mid-1970s. It is not fanciful to see culture management ideas as being a response to what was becoming a pervasive crisis of confidence. At all events, it represented

---

1   Needless to say, this was a wildly optimistic picture of the Japanese economy in the 1970s and 1980s. It depicted, at the very best, life in the big corporations. That life was much harder than might be imagined, but for sure it was nothing when compared with the Japanese economy in general. During the Japanese 'economic miracle' probably three-quarters of the economy was not in the big companies but in its subcontractors who used migrant labour in camps where conditions were extraordinarily harsh. See Kamata (1982) for a horrifying account of the realities of what made the Japanese economy competitive. Current 'competitive pressures' derive from, and are used to justify, unregulated 'export processing zones' in the Developing World where beatings, torture of trade unionists and sub-subsistence wages are the norm (see Klein, 2000), and from progressively degraded conditions for the working class in the Developed World (see Perelman, 2005).

part of what the historian Robert Locke (1996) has incisively identified as the 'collapse of the American management mystique'.

The mystique of American management was born out of American
military success in the Second World War. The landings in Normandy,
in particular, represented a huge logistical achievement, and it was these
logistics which were thought to characterize the superiority of
American management. However, whilst not denying the significance of
the American war effort, nor the huge sacrifices made in the Normandy
landings, it is also the case that an important, and perhaps over-riding,
reason for the victory in Western Europe was that the cream of the
German army had been defeated by the Soviet Union on the Eastern
front where an estimated 20 million Soviet soldiers and civilians died.
Without rehearsing these issues in detail, suffice to say that it is far from
clear that American logistics were as central to their military success as
had been believed in the immediate post-war period.

There were some other strands in American culture which helped
to explain the popularity of the culture approach. America had been
in the vanguard of the youthful counter-culture which emerged, especially on the West coast, in the 1960s. Those involved or influenced
by it were, by the early 1980s, in their thirties and coming to positions of influence in organizations. The backwash of this movement
may well have created a climate in which talk of empowerment and
harmony had an appeal which at other times it might have lacked,
for as Boltanski and Chiapello (2007) explain, the new managerialism took over much of the language of the 1960s protest movement.
And similar points could perhaps be made about the increasing
acceptance of feminism and of women in organizations, which
helped to foster a receptive atmosphere for what could be read by
some as a move away from the macho management of more
traditional approaches.

Regardless of the exact part played by these and other factors, my
point is that the emergence and take-up of ideas about organizational
culture happened within historical, economic and cultural contexts
and was neither inevitable nor fortuitous. As I have repeatedly
stressed, organization theory can never be separated from such contexts, and cannot be thought of as simply unfolding through some
kind of natural or logical progression. Nor was it the case that the
basic ideas of organizational culture had never been articulated before
the 1980s – it is their widespread take-up which was lacking, presumably for lack of a context within which it made sense to do so. By the
1980s there existed, at least in the US but also, with local twists, in

the UK and elsewhere, that mixture of fear and hope that made a fertile soil for the embrace of culture management.

And embrace it they did. Culture was *the* word within organizations for the next two decades, and it continues to be part of the routine repertoire of managers and of organizational theorists to the present day. It's fair to say that some of the shine has gone off it – both through familiarity and because, as I will discuss in a minute, it has not really lived up to its promises – but the basic analysis of organizations that culture management contained remains at the heart of current managerial thinking, as we will see not just in this chapter but in the two that follow it, notwithstanding the limitations of the techniques it proposes. Indeed, one index of those limitations is that of the 62 'excellent' companies profiled in Peters and Waterman's book, a large number had within a year ceased to meet the criteria of excellence, and within a few years, some had ceased to exist altogether. Perhaps that is not surprising in what the late Peter Drucker witheringly called the 'book for juveniles'; yet hundreds of similar books, typically extolling the virtues of one particular company at one particular time, were produced and sold in the following decades and form the basis of the endless case studies of 'best practice' used on management courses throughout the world. Hmm.

doing culture

Shallow as it undoubtedly was, the culture idea proposes more than that organizations should develop shared values. Rather, it identifies a whole range of organizational practices designed to elicit these values. And whilst the idea may have been shallow, the practices it promoted had as their aim, and sometimes their effect, something like the reconstitution of personhood. In Chapter 2 I talked about the ways in which human relations theory initiated a new domain for management in which people – or more accurately personhood – became a target for intervention and reshaping. In many respects culture management stands in this tradition, but I think that it entails a noticeable refinement and extension of it. Culture management is much more ambitious in its desire to shape people's beliefs than 'traditional' human relations. The latter tried, certainly, to 'adjust' employees to their workplace, but it also sought to design work around what were assumed to be a relatively stable and enduring set of human needs. The search for shared values entails a much more aggressive design agenda in which it is the worker, not the work, which is the main locus of management. Culture management aspires to intervene in and regulate being, so that there is no distance between individuals' purposes and those of the organization for which they work.

Some of the more obvious ways in which this is done include selection of staff who are, or appear to be, amenable to organizational values and, perhaps more controversially, the sacking of those existing employees who are not so amenable. Since culture management typically accompanies a 'downsizing' of managerial numbers, the opportunities for such sackings certainly exist. The application of culture management was very much at the heart of the changes brought by the large-scale privatizations of publicly owned organizations in the UK and elsewhere in the 1980s and 1990s. In addition to changing ownership, there was an agenda to shift the organizations from a public sector 'ethos' (or culture), which was presumed to be inefficient, towards a more business-like orientation. At the same time, there was an imperative to cut costs through redundancy. Thus many of those who were targeted for, or who took up offers of, redundancy were those who were unwilling or unable to 'commit' to the new culture. However, one difficulty of such an approach is that it may well (and in the case of the privatizations undoubtedly did) strip out those with the greatest degree of technical knowledge and experience of the services they offered. It is, for this and many other reasons, highly questionable whether privatization did very much for the effectiveness of service provision, as anyone who has travelled on a train in the UK in the last few years is likely to realize.

But the adjustment of personnel according to who fits in is only the most superficial, and least novel, of the techniques which culture management brings to bear. More insidious is the use of all kinds of training, communication and what Peters and Waterman, with characteristic banality, called 'hoopla'. Employees are exposed to organizational values in the form of videos, mission statements, pocket-sized cards with core values printed upon them, company slogans, company songs, group exercises and a whole gamut of ever-more weird and wonderful happenings such as, in one UK bank, parades of employees in animal costumes chanting the virtues of the bank as a fun place to be!

This I think is pretty bizarre stuff, and perhaps of necessity it has to be. One interpretation of what is going on here is an attempt to produce Hawthorne effects of the sort discussed in Chapter 2. But these effects (as the Hawthorne Studies themselves showed) are short-lived. Therefore a search for novelty will always be needed to keep the momentum going. But, more importantly, most of the more extravagant examples of culture management need to operate at a symbolic level. Culture, after all, is not a tangible thing. We learn about cultures (whether societal or organizational) as it were indirectly – through the meaning which events appear to have. For example, the animal parade *symbolizes* the zany culture which it supposedly obtains. The manipulation of symbols provides some of the deepest techniques of culture management.

Company names and logos are an obvious example as these in some sense represent or symbolize the whole of the organization, both projecting it to the outer world of its markets and back into the organization in the form of its employees. It is no coincidence that the privatizations provide good examples of this. To take just one, Yorkshire Electricity Board became Yorkshire Electricity after privatization. Why? Because 'board' sounds old-fashioned, bureaucratic, public sectorish. But Yorkshire Electricity soon became YE, which sounds altogether more snazzy and less parochial. It also has the advantage of not really telling you what the company does, which it is handy given that these organizations quickly diversified into non-traditional activities (handy, too, when the diversification embraces both electricity and water which don't in real, if not corporate, life mix too well). Such developments are also an aspect of the wider ways in which companies are increasingly detached from localities and communities, as discussed in detail in Chapter 5.

These shifting organizational identities clearly relate to attempts to shift employee identities, but of course they don't necessarily do so. More profound symbolic manipulations relate to things like architecture and clothing. One of the persistent ways in which shared values have been symbolized has been the erosion of many of the symbols of hierarchy in organizations like separate offices (instead of open plan), different floors of the building for different grades, differential access to parking, company cars and so on. In the motor industry, in particular, one idea imported from Japan in the 1980s was to have employees at all levels up to and including senior management wearing identical boiler suits, and all attending 'morning assemblies', which sometimes included the singing of company hymns. The symbolism of this is quite profound: it seems to say that 'we' are all working for a common cause, each playing our own parts within it, but all parts equally valued, and the quasi-religious aspects are easy to see.

Then there are the hosts of rituals and stories designed to impact upon how people feel (an important word) about the organization. The supermarket boss whose childhood was spent selling cheap eggs from his satchel – symbolizing his lifelong commitment to good value groceries. The Honda worker, referred to in Peters and Waterman, who on passing a Honda in the street will straighten its windscreen wipers because he cannot bear to see an imperfect Honda, symbolizing the commitment of Honda workers to quality (I find this story particularly creepy). The hotel receptionist who, finding the hotel full, invites a desperate late-night arrival to stay in her spare room, symbolizing the commitment of the hotel chain's staff to its customers (that's pretty twee, as well). The New York advertising agency, described in a brilliant article by Michael Rosen (1988), which has a Christmas sketch show ritual in which senior managers are lampooned, symbolizing the democracy and informality of the firm. And the legions of organizations which have a 'dress-down Friday' to symbolize the unstuffy, egalitarian culture they purport to have (at least on Fridays).

The list goes on, and although each example in isolation perhaps doesn't mean much, their accumulation within an individual organization tends towards building – more or less convincingly – a story about the culture to which employees are invited to subscribe. But perhaps 'invited' is the wrong word (revealingly, attendance at the Christmas party Rosen describes was compulsory). First, because there are real sanctions on those who fail to do so – if you don't fit in, then you may well be first in line for the next set of redundancies. However, that, whilst true, isn't really so important as the fact that, rather than being an invitation to be accepted or refused, the most profound forms of culture management circumvent choice. In what is to my mind probably the finest study of organizational culture management – Gideon Kunda's book *Engineering Culture* – one of the managers of the firm studied gives this chilling explanation: 'The idea is to educate people without them knowing it. Have the religion and not know how they got it' (Kunda, 1992: 5).

This underlines what has to be grasped in thinking about culture management. Its whole purpose is to reconstitute beliefs – nothing less will do if its promise of the removal of supervision is to be achieved. In its sophisticated manifestations it uses techniques by no means dissimilar to those of religious cults.

what's wrong with all this?

I don't really know where to start. I suppose the most obvious question is to ask whether cultures really can be managed in this way. From the very early days of the culture frenzy there were voices saying that it could not. Linda Smircich (1983) was one of the first of these. She suggested that organizational culture could be thought of in at least two ways. In one version, culture was a 'critical variable', in another a 'root metaphor'. What she meant by the first term (I'll come back to the second later) was that culture management assumed that culture could indeed be managed – that it was amenable to intervention, control and definition, that it was a critical variable. This was clearly the assumption of those who advocated it. After all, to write about culture management but then admit that it wasn't actually manageable would be slightly odd. But it is plain that these advocates had much more in mind than the proposition that culture could be managed. Pascale and Athos had talked about shared values as one of the 'levers' of management and they clearly believed that culture could be treated as if it were part of an organizational machine in which controls were manipulated at the whim of managers.

So culture management says more than that culture can be controlled. It also proposes that it be controlled in particular directions. After all, shared values or strong culture don't say anything at all about what those values are, or what that strength consists of. For example, we might envisage an organization in which the employees had shared values that said that they should sit around drinking tea. But would this be the kind of organization anticipated by the culture management advocates? I think we can say that the answer is 'no'. More than that, we can say that *of course* the answer is 'no'. Culture management imagines a world in which shared values are directed towards the goal of productivity, whether as quantity or quality. So, suddenly, the freedom and empowerment envisaged by culture management takes on a new hue: these supposedly progressive goals are only on offer if the employees accept that their efforts must be directed towards the profitability of the company. One index of this is the way that, although in principle, a culture specifies what is *distinctive* about an organization, in practice the cultures sought by organizations involve a very limited and extremely repetitive set of pieties: customer service, quality, flexibility and innovation being the watchwords. Why? Because these are the attributes which senior managers believe will deliver competitive advantage.

And this is the thing about culture management. It is based upon the idea that cultural values are hierarchically defined, that is defined by senior managers or by head office. Linda Smircich's analysis says that there is a different way of viewing culture. Culture as root metaphor, as Smircich dubs it, says that, yes, organizations have cultures but that these are spontaneous, unmanaged, just the way things are. It is a culture, certainly, but it doesn't necessarily conform to what managers want. Culture as root metaphor means something the organization *is* rather than something it *has*. People in organizations do things, they work together in a certain way: that's the culture. It is natural, spontaneous and, in short, it is what it is.

This is a nice dichotomy that has been influential in the literature and which captures something of the reality of organizations – two things that don't always go together, by the way. But where does it take us? For some analysts, of whom Meek (1988) is perhaps the most articulate, the answer is that since culture is just what it is, then it is relatively impervious to intervention. A good way of thinking about this is in terms of stories. Of course it is true that stories go round organizations and that these define something of the culture. But it doesn't follow that the stories manufactured and put around by culture managers gain much purchase. These are normally cringe-inducing stories about sycophantic employees giving great service. As such, they don't have much chance of being taken seriously when compared with more grounded stories about how, say, a manager never turns up for work and relies upon subordinates to cover for him (or her; no, let's say it's him).

So there is a 'real', spontaneous culture and a 'managed', imposed culture on top of this. And this means that attempts by managers to speak lightly of changing 'the culture' have to be treated as, at best, no more than optimism. There is plenty of evidence to back up this jaundiced analysis. In an interesting paper, Ogbonna and Wilkinson (1988) look at supermarket staff. The staff were encouraged to embrace a corporate culture of 'customer service', which entailed smiling at customers and being friendly so as to make them feel valued. The studies showed that the staff did not embrace the culture management programme, but did conform superficially to its demands. They 'smiled but did not mean it' and did so because they were aware that cameras and mystery shoppers were checking on them.

Now this is very revealing study. You might think that, if the staff are doing what is expected of them by 'the culture', then culture management has succeeded. But of course a moment's thought shows that this is not true. For culture management requires that staff 'really' believe in the values, not just that they go along with them in case a camera found that they were not smiling. And it requires it not just for some theoretical reason but because unless staff really embrace the customer service culture then the costs of managing and monitoring them will not be saved.

Let me give a sharper example, again from supermarkets. I once had a part-time MBA student who was a senior manager in a supermarket chain which was known as an exemplar of successful culture management, and featured on management courses as a good practice case study in this area. This case study presented survey evidence to show the wide extent of buy-in to corporate culture values. My student wanted to test the extent to which front-line staff subscribed to these corporate values. The staff had just been subject to a multi-million pound culture training initiative. My student found, not that staff did not believe in the values, but that three-quarters of them claimed never to have *heard* of the values.

This kind of example really needs to be taken seriously for two reasons. One, which is the most important for this chapter, is that attempts at culture management don't necessarily work. And perhaps they particularly don't work when the targets are low-paid workers in front-line positions. It makes little financial sense to devote huge resources to their cultural training – most are temporary and part-time workers – even though they are the ones who interact with customers. So the typical approach is to show them a video or two and hope for the best. The second thing we should take from this example is that many of those exciting case studies which management courses urge upon their students are, well, kind of crap. They reflect what managers say about organizations, not – or not necessarily – the lived experience of those who work in them.

So, if we are sensible, we will be sceptical about the more grandiose claims of culture management. Does this mean we can ignore them altogether? No, for attempts to manage culture *are* part of organizational culture and can't be discounted so lightly. Although that supermarket example suggests that culture management may have relatively little purchase, it doesn't follow that this is necessarily the case. Kunda's study of the engineering firm 'Tech' is a good example of this, because it shows how the values promoted by culture management do get taken up and used in everyday practice and language by the firm's employees. Kunda does show, however, that the way in which this happens is much more mixed and ambiguous than the proponents of culture management recognize.

For these reasons, it is important to tread a path which, whilst duly suspicious of the claims that culture can be unproblematically managed, avoids lapsing into 'cultural purism'. This is the term given by my former colleague Hugh Willmott in his landmark paper on organizational culture management (Willmott, 1993). He believes that culture management has to be taken seriously because of the potential it offers to reformulate identity and meaning in line with managerial *diktat*. His suggestion, and it is one made by several analysts of culture, is that it is a particular form of control which seeks to operate not by the external regulation of behaviour, but by shaping the internal world, the identity, of people at work. I share this view, and it is implicit in what I have already written. But Willmott goes rather further than this, in making a comparison between culture management and George Orwell's (1949) brilliant fictional description of a future totalitarian society in the novel *Nineteen Eighty-Four*.

I have perhaps already prefigured this by talking about the way that values are defined hierarchically in organizational culture, but there is more to it than that. In *Nineteen Eighty-Four*, Orwell draws upon his knowledge of the totalitarian regimes of Nazi Germany and the Stalinist Soviet Union (and, it seems, interestingly in this context, from his reading of Burnham's account of the managerial revolution – see Orwell, 1946) to point to certain features of such regimes. These include, famously, 'Big Brother', better known in the UK now as the name of a TV programme which observes a group of fairly awful people in the hope (often realized) that they will do something gross. Orwell's Big Brother is the patriarchal dictator who constantly monitors members of society for incorrect behaviour (it is this theme of surveillance, of course, which links the Orwell novel with the TV show). This behaviour is not confined to overt subversion but to departures from orthodoxy of any sort. Part and parcel of this is a language, 'Newspeak', which by refining the range of what can be expressed places ever-more restricted limits around what can be thought. The society is characterized by monstrous, counter-intuitive slogans, such as 'freedom is slavery', the invocation of enemy hordes which will destroy the society and an emphasis, for members of the Party, on communal activities and the abnegation of the individual in favour of the collective good.

I think – and here I am going further than Willmott, and probably being less subtle – that there are many parallels to be drawn between

Orwell's nightmare vision of the future and culture management. In culture management, there is very often the construction of a heroic leader (it is noteworthy that many culture management stories concern such leaders) and there is intensive use of surveillance methods. One of the richest veins of organization theory in recent years has been the use of the 'post-structuralist' ideas of Michel Foucault (1979) to explore surveillance at work. Foucault famously analysed the panoptic prison in which prisoners could be watched but would not know when they were being watched. Over time, such a situation would lead to the prisoners becoming self-disciplining. I will come back to this in a moment, but just to continue the parallels with *Nineteen Eighty-Four*, culture management is very much concerned with promoting corporate languages and slogans, and typically encourages employees to believe that 'the competition' will destroy the organization if they are not compliant to managerial demands.

More than anything – and this is more Hugh Willmott's point – totalitarianism, as in *Nineteen Eighty-Four*, invokes the collectivity and elevates this above the individual. The individual both matters less than the collective but, also, finds him or herself through alignment with and subservience to the collective. This was certainly a feature of both Nazi and Stalinist regimes, as well as of other cases of totalitarian society. Culture management, in a similar way, impinges on autonomy but, in an insidious twist, claims that it actually promotes autonomy ('freedom is slavery'). This is the nexus of issues around empowerment. As I suggested earlier, empowerment in organizations has the curious feature that it is only allowed if it is exercised in ways beneficial to the organization. Willmott makes the more general point that empowerment cannot meaningfully be *bestowed* upon others but can only be meaningful if it is *achieved* by people themselves.

How seriously should we take all this? I'm not quite sure. There are some fairly obvious limitations to the analogy with *Nineteen Eighty-Four*. In the novel, the central character, Winston Smith, is taken to a torture chamber, subjected to grotesque violence and has his character reprogrammed through sophisticated psychological techniques. Someone who resists an organizational culture is not going to be treated this way. At worst, they will be sacked. Relatedly, people can choose whether they work for an organization which manages its culture; people in totalitarian societies typically cannot. But this isn't quite the end of the story. People in our society do suffer economically and in other ways if they do not work, and most large companies do use some form of culture management (still, people could work for a small company, or be self-employed). And we can certainly imagine some people – perhaps those who are relatively old, with poor chances of being employed elsewhere and with a family to support – enduring a certain amount of humiliation and bullying rather than lose their job. Even so, it is important, not least because of the need not to blunt our wariness of full-blown totalitarianism, to see that this is an imperfect analogy, even if it captures a certain reality.

surveillance, choice and self-management

I want to talk about this a little more by returning to the issue of surveillance. There is much more to Foucault's work than the panoptic prison, and much more that is of great significance for organization theory (particularly good explanations of this are Knights, 1992, and Burrell, 1988). This leads some of those who are interested in Foucault to be rather sniffy about the way that so much attention has been given to 'panopticism'. But I disagree. Surveillance is an important part of people's organizational experience – and was recognized as such long before Foucault's work – and the panopticon is a very illuminating way of exploring it. There are many examples. In wider society, examples include CCTV cameras, marketing databases, mobile phone tracking and DNA databases. In the workplace, it is becoming increasingly common to track employees' movements through smart cards. The supermarket 'mystery shopper' mentioned earlier is another case. The way that call centre operators have their calls monitored to check that they are using the right words, and dealing with the call at maximum speed is another, as is the measurement of call throughput.

Of course there are plenty of other examples of surveillance too, but the last of those just given are relevant for two reasons. One is that they are linked, specifically, to culture (for example, and especially, cultures promoting the value of customer service). The other is that they are cases not just of surveillance but of panoptic surveillance, in the sense that people don't know whether or not they are being observed at any particular time – so-called discontinuous surveillance. This is important as it is this which leads to the proposition of self-management through the internalization of norms of working. Other forms of surveillance – the entire genre of activities called 'overseeing' – do not necessarily have this quality in that they are continuous rather than discontinuous. This means that they work, if they do work, on the basis of compliance with external regulation, and the assumption is that if the overseeing ceases then so too does the compliance. This is certainly a form of control but it is not one which can be used to support the claim that culture management represents an insidious reshaping of the self. What is perhaps surprising at first glance is that continuous surveillance, for all that it may be considered irksome, is actually less disciplinary in Foucauldian terms than discontinuous surveillance, in that the former remains external monitoring whereas the latter becomes, potentially, internalized.

One of the most widely quoted studies in this vein is Sewell and Wilkinson's (1992) paper on surveillance in an electronics factory. They argue that new manufacturing techniques, especially those involving total quality management (TQM) and just-in-time management (JIT), which are linked to the promotion of a culture of quality, offer particularly intense forms of surveillance, both electronically and through the peer pressure imposed by teams, leading to the self-imposition of high output levels. Sewell and Wilkinson spend a lot of time explaining the ways in which the workplace is like a panoptic prison. Actually the original design for the prison, by Jeremy Bentham, was inspired by the workshop run by Bentham's brother. The model therefore derives from the workplace in the first instance.

But that is a detail. The key question is whether, either in the prison or in the workplace, surveillance does in fact lead to self-regulating behaviour. Sewell and Wilkinson have been criticized for presenting too deterministic a picture of surveillance, as if its existence has a necessary effect in terms of self-regulation. On the one hand, it may be that people do not in fact work as hard as they can, but find all kinds of ways of getting round surveillance systems. On the other hand, even if they do work as hard as they can, it does not follow that this is because they have internalized disciplines, just that they are scared of getting caught out. By extension, this whole genre of work has been criticized for a lack of attention to the ways in which people in organizations resist or subvert control, somewhat ironically given the fact that resistance was one of Foucault's major preoccupations.

This clearly relates back to the earlier issue about the extent to which culture management can be thought of as analogous to totalitarianism and corrosive of autonomy and choice. The totalitarian analogy would suppose that resistance would be very limited (although, as the observed realities of totalitarian regimes suggest, never entirely absent). At a more theoretical level this is illuminated by an exchange between the sociologist Anthony Giddens, who tends to be sceptical of Foucauldian claims, and the organization theorist Gibson Burrell, who was one of those who first applied post-structuralist analysis to the study of organizations. Giddens (1984) argues that Foucault's work rests on the over-extension of what applies in 'total institutions' (for example, prisons, poorhouses, the army) to organizations in general. This ignores the rather specific features of total institutions, the most obvious being that you cannot normally leave them, and spend your entire life inside them. This is likely to mean that the kinds of subjects or identities produced within them will be of a rather unusual kind. Burrell's (1988) counter to this argument is summed up by the interesting observation that whilst we may not spend our lives in total organizations, the organization of our lives is total. In other words, that there is no escape from living in an organized way, and this inevitably impinges upon our subjectivity. This is a more deterministic argument, in that it suggests little opportunity for choice and no possibility of meaningful escape.

In line with my general aim of accessibility I have not done anything like justice to the complexities of this debate, but I hope that I have given enough indication of its main contours. It is not, of course, possible to make a final pronouncement on what is the right answer. But my feeling, for what little it is worth, is that what is at issue here is a need to think in a much more subtle way about what is entailed in choice than is normal, either in organization theory or elsewhere. Consider the objection to thinking of culture management as totalitarian being that people can choose to leave the organization if they wish. The point, though, is not that culture management is totalitarian because it holds on to people who want to leave (and in this regard, it *is* different to totalitarian states); it is that it exerts a hold over people such that they do not wish to do so. The evidence for totalitarianism, therefore, is not confounded by the existence of choice but by the way in which that choice is used.

Developing from Foucault's work, both on subjectivity in general and on governmentality in particular (Foucault, 1991), Nikolas Rose has presented an analysis of the way that self-governing subjects emerge as 'entrepreneurs of themselves, shaping their own lives through the choices they make among the forms of life open to them' (Rose, 1989: 226) so that 'the Citizen, in work as much as outside it, is engaged in a project to shape his or her life as an autonomous individual driven by motives of self-fulfilment' (1989: 115). However, the contemporary preoccupation with choice has a distinct irony for, as Strathern (1992) points out, in such cultures we have no choice but to make choices. Not only this, but the consequences of our choices will be our own responsibility. You've had a heart attack? You shouldn't have chosen to eat so much fatty food. Not enough pension? You should have chosen to save more. Failed your exams? You should have chosen to work harder. In these senses, choice is to be understood not in terms of the expression of freedom, but as a disciplining and 'responsibilizing' process whose power is obscured, or, rather, magnified by the sense it gives of freedom (a point I will take up again in a different context in Chapter 5). Choice is therefore not an alternative to control, but rather, the way in which we exercise choices is expressive of control, including, most especially, those things which we do not experience as choice but understand to be 'just the way things are'.

From this perspective, the issue of the panopticon and surveillance also looks rather different. I don't at all want to decry the attention which has been paid to organizational surveillance mechanisms, which are real, important and often oppressive. However, they tend to think about the panopticon in rather literal ways – as physical (even if, often, 'virtual') artefacts. I think that a more important implication comes if we think about the panopticon metaphorically. The surveillance studies *do* use the panopticon metaphorically when they say something along the lines of 'the call centre is *like* the panoptic prison', but they treat it as if it were a discrete 'thing' rather than a kind of nebulous idea. It then becomes something contestable, resistible or embraceable. But what seems more profound to me are those parts of our taken for granted which disappear from sight as things to be contested, resisted or embraced. These constitute the important stuff; because then the choices happen by default.

Imagine a group of students sitting in the lecture hall, taking notes. Of course they have a choice; they could leave, they could not take notes. And of course they are subject to disciplines (registers, tests) which would tend to prevent them doing so. Sometimes they don't turn up; sometimes they don't take notes – their behaviour isn't determined by the existence of those disciplines and they sometimes resist them. But they could also burst into song or remove all their clothes. And this they never do (or not in my experience, anyway). They don't need to *think* not to do so, and thus although they are making a choice they do not experience it as such. It is these taken-for-granted choices which form part of the fabric of our being which seem to me to be expressive of the more profound forms of self-discipline, and it presumably derives from strongly embedded socialization processes which exist (although of course in different forms and with different outcomes) in all societies. These deep and diffuse socialization processes are the important sense, I think, in which our lives are totally in organizations and in which panoptic metaphors have their most important purchase.

In terms of the workplace, people's behaviour is clearly proscribed in the same way as it is in the lecture theatre – there are a range of basic, obvious behaviours which we discipline ourselves about. Their obviousness makes them boring, perhaps even invisible, but from my point of view it is what makes them interesting and important. Many of these disciplines are quite general, nothing to do with the workplace at all. Others are more specific – our acceptance that we should turn up more or less on time and do more or less what we are told (and, sure, some people manage neither of these things). Both general and specific cases are an outcome of socialization, and also no doubt an ongoing medium of socialization (in the sense that our adherence to prescribed behaviours is reinforced by the constant observation of how others behave).

So, then, what about culture management? The point, I think, is that this too attempts a socialization process with a view to prescribing and proscribing behaviour through the adoption of certain values. Culture management proposes a version of 'the way things are' and invites us to take it as so. Indeed, it is surely no coincidence that one of the most commonly used and easily remembered definitions of organizational culture – so ubiquitous that it is attributed to all kinds of authors – is 'the way we do things around here'.

For this reason, culture management deserves to be criticized because it is indeed an attempt to gain an insidious form of control. It may be that socialization processes are in some sense necessary in any society; it doesn't follow that these processes should be aimed at binding the individual into the attempt to gain competitive advantage for the organizations they work for. For sure, what culture management does in this regard is sometimes clumsy and ineffective. But I don't think we should judge it less harshly just because it isn't very good at its job or is attempted on the cheap. If it is an attempt to exert insidious control, is it any better if it fails to do so?

Anyway, if we're looking at an insidious control of what is defined as normal or natural, maybe culture management isn't so ineffective. I've mentioned some of the studies which show that culture management can regulate identity and the way people treat some things as natural and normal. It's very likely the case that those most liable to be affected in this way are not the rank and file employees like supermarket workers and call centre operatives, but more senior people – the managers and professionals in organizations. This is an interesting idea, because it suggests that what is at stake in culture management is not a kind of managerial domination of the working classes. Let me try to explain. Much conventional organization theory sees the workforce as in need of control, direction and co-ordination, and devises various ways of achieving this, of which culture management may be one such. It is assumed that managers themselves are already committed to organizational goals and values – at a basic level, that they will work hard and act responsibly. This conventional view has an ironic counterpart amongst some more radical commentators, who see the working classes as subject to the power of managers acting in ways perfectly in tune with the profit-seeking motives of their shareholders (Braverman, 1974).

Yet, as I suggested in Chapter 2, management had to be 'made' responsible, and at many periods in time this could not be assumed. What now appears quite normal and natural is that managers will work long hours, do whatever needs to be done to get the job done and are motivated to do so by the intrinsic interest of their work, the payment they receive and, in general, a sense of responsibility and professionalism. That same professionalism, unsurprisingly, informs the conduct of, precisely, professionals like doctors, lawyers and accountants – even academics. We don't think of these people as being 'empowered to delight the customer' or enrolled in 'joy gangs' (to use one of the ugliest pieces of culture-speak). Yet it is they who have most obviously taken to heart a set of norms about values and behaviour, learned, certainly, through general education, but also through the organizational processes of their workplaces, professional associations and so on. Of course this doesn't mean that such people never betray trust, are never lazy or even corrupt. But, to a very large extent, they exhibit a great deal of the self-management associated with culture management, and the occasions where they do not do so are remarkable as a result.

As I write these words it is a Sunday afternoon, and I have been working all weekend. I am on sabbatical in France and there is absolutely no one who knows or cares whether I am working or not. On some of my work I have imposed deadlines to meet, but for this book the deadlines are hazy and some way off. But I am still working, rather than doing any of the other things I could do with my weekend. Why? The obvious answer is because I choose to do so. That's true – but that is the whole point of the earlier discussion I gave about choice. It's the way I exercise choice which makes me self-managed, and that self-management is both part of my own identity and a part of the occupational and organizational cultures of academics.

This is not necessarily a 'bad thing'. It gets books written (well, that may not be such great news), it keeps organizations going, it delivers medical care in a responsible way and so on. But that isn't really the point. After all, the loyalty of party members in totalitarian regimes keeps the system going and is often associated with spectacular feats of industrial progress and military conquest which, at least for members of such societies, may be seen as no 'bad thing'. So the point is, more, to see how culture does exert a power – a power to produce values and behaviour.

In any case, 'not necessarily' are big words. The cultural production of self-management is, I would suggest, something present in and perhaps necessary to all social relations, although for sure the form it will take varies. The key issue is the way that this culture is developed and the uses to which it is put. I suppose this is another version of the question of instrumental and substantive rationality, discussed in Chapter 1. Cultures which develop through time, negotiation and which are put to uses that have some kind of dignity and substantive value are one thing, and perhaps some of the professions are examples of this. But culture management in modern organizations typically has few of these characteristics. It develops not through time and negotiation but as a 'programme' devised by a small number of people and projected onto other people either as an imposition or (more effectively) through guile. Moreover, it proposes a use which seems to lack dignity and value. It invokes the bastardized language of a counter-culture animated by a desire for individual freedom in the service of organizational conformity. To invite or seduce people to devote their whole being to producing cars, hamburgers or insurance policies seems to me a substantial negation of the possibilities that human existence might otherwise have. That these tawdry schemes often fail to secure their aims is a testimony to the good sense of those exposed to them, but in no way negates the presumption and arrogance of those devising them.

◼◼◼◼◼◼ conclusion

In this chapter I have tried to think through one of the central issues in contemporary organization. What I mean to imply by calling it that is the idea that 'culture' is not simply a specific topic within organization theory but is more like the *leitmotif* of a whole assembly of recent ways in which organizations have developed. Take any example – total quality management, business process re-engineering, the learning organization or the generic case of 'post-bureaucracy' discussed in the next chapter – and you will find an appeal to the need to create an appropriate organizational culture. Moreover, culture, like all these other examples, is crucially concerned with the promotion of self-managing, self-disciplined individuals.

This represents both an obvious continuation of, but also something of a break with, the classical approaches to organization theory. It is a continuation in that it picks up on and develops the human relations concerned with personhood as a focus for managerial attention and as an organizational resource. Moreover, as this implies, it exemplifies the themes identified in the previous chapters of a preoccupation with instrumental rationality and control. It is a break in the scale of its ambitions with respect to self-management. It would certainly be wrong to ignore that self-management was an aim of many older approaches, most obviously human relations theory. However, even the latter remained connected to a wider project for 'external' management since, as I suggested in Chapter 2, it was at least in part related to the promotion of a managerial elite with expertise in human relations. For sure the contemporary approaches create expert elites – consultants and managers with know-how in culture – but they also run alongside the erosion of the large cadre of middle managers, discussed in Chapter 5. Thus, the focus on the 'internal management' of the individual is all the more relentless, for culture management promotes management just as it demotes managers.

But for all that culture has been central to recent organizational theory and practice, it is only one part of a matrix of wider developments. These purport to represent a fundamental change in which the basic template of bureaucratic organization is in the process of being displaced by a new form – post-bureaucracy – which is required by the supposedly unprecedented changes of the contemporary world. In the next chapter I will explore this brave new world.

4

Post-Bureaucracy and Change Management

The future is made of the same stuff as the present.
Simone Weil

As many readers of this book will be aware, there has in recent years been a war going on. I am not talking about war in Iraq, Afghanistan or even the nebulous 'war on terror' (and how depressing it is that this sentence has not had to be removed for the second edition of this book). I am talking about the war against bureaucracy. Much of the debate around organizational culture can be seen as a campaign in this war, but it has now spread across many battlefields and is reported on in almost every recent book about organizations and management. Open any of them and you will find, in some form or other, a very similar argument. It says that a bureaucratic way of organizing is one bound up with tasks of a particular kind. Specifically, it is found in situations where very large numbers of identical, standard operations are needed – processing social security claims or mass-producing cars, for example. It suits situations where a rigid chain of command is favoured, where little training or initiative is required since all that people need to do is to follow rules and orders. Finally, it suits situations where there is little rapid change in the organization's environment.

Conventional wisdom says that these kinds of conditions no longer obtain or, at any rate, are increasingly rare. Since at least the 1970s, but with a growing insistence, it has been claimed that such 'industrial' (or 'Fordist') conditions are giving way to a 'post-industrial' (or 'post-Fordist') era. This argument takes many forms but in essence it says that the economy has moved from the mass production of standard products towards short product runs for niche markets. At the same time, it is suggested that people in organizations need – and perhaps want – to be more flexible and innovative, rather than simply following orders. Finally, it is held that the environment of all or most organizations has become increasingly unstable and prone to rapid change.

Against that background, the argument goes on, there has been a development of a range of new organizational forms. These are given many different names – the virtual, networked or even postmodern organization – but as an umbrella term we can call them 'post-bureaucracies'. Charles Heckscher (1994) goes so far as to assert that it is possible to identify a post-bureaucratic ideal-type, in contrast to Weber's ideal-type of bureaucracy. In outline, it consists of the following characteristics:

- Rules are replaced with consensus and dialogue based upon personal influence rather than status. People are trusted to act on the basis of shared values rather than rules.
- Responsibilities are assigned on the basis of competence for tasks rather than hierarchy, and are treated as individuals rather than impersonally.
- The organization has an open boundary, so that rather than full-time permanent employment, people come into and out of the organization in a flexible way including part-time, temporary and consultancy arrangements. Work is no longer done in fixed hours or at a designated place.

It's easy to pick out two things from this description. One is that it does indeed run counter to all of the precepts of bureaucracy, although like much that is contemporary in organization theory, it grows out of the classical approaches. Rules, hierarchy, career structures, impersonality are all swept away. The other is that this represents both a re-articulation of, and a departure from, the ideas about culture management. A re-articulation because of its stress on shared values. And a departure because it envisages not a fixed collective of organizationally socialized and disciplined (or 'empowered') employees but a floating complement of staff only intermittently and perhaps fleetingly associated with the organization. So it takes over all of the problems of the culture model but it also adds some new ones. For if it is questionable whether an organization can inculcate 'shared values' in its workforce, then how much more questionable must it be for such values to obtain within such transitory attachments?

There are several ways in which we can and should mock and deride this kind of thinking. One, which I will come back to later in this chapter, is the cod history and sociology which informs this kind of 'new era' thinking. The way that Heckscher positions his 'ideal type' as being on all fours with Weber's analysis of bureaucracy – founded as it was on massive and sustained scholarship – is actually the least objectionable. Heckscher is at least a serious and committed researcher, and compared with most of those who trot out this kind of line a sophisticated and insightful reasoner. But consider the work of Hammer and Champy (1993) who so influentially propounded the 'business process re-engineering revolution'. This too represents itself as an anti-bureaucratic creed (although, as even its name implies, it retains the imprint of the engineering approach of the most traditional versions of management).

But unlike Heckscher, only the flimsiest of research is invoked to sustain the grandiloquent claim that re-engineering is comparable in scope and profundity with Adam Smith's discovery (sic) of the division of labour (Hammer and Champy, 1993: 5). This is the kind of 'epochal' claim which du Gay (2003) identifies as typical of the war on bureaucracy.

A second way of pricking the presumption of the post-bureaucratic case is one which carefully documents just how flimsy its reality claims are. Paul Thompson and his collaborators, through a series of detailed studies both of aggregate statistical evidence and individual cases, have shown that job structures and work experiences have been remarkably unaltered by the post-bureaucratic revolution. They suggest that its claims have conflated several different trends so that whereas the rise of the service economy is an undoubted trend in advanced industrial societies, what it typically means is the growth of low-skilled and standardized jobs in, for example, catering, telesales and call centres (Warhurst and Thompson, 1998). From a similar kind of perspective, Rick Delbridge's work – which is one of the best recent contributions to a distinguished tradition of workplace ethnographies – has called into question the extent of post-bureaucratic transformation (Delbridge, 1998).

The study reports on Delbridge's time in two British factories. One is a Japanese-owned electronics plant (Nippon CTV), the other a European-owned producer of automotive components (ValleyCo). Although strictly speaking this is not a study of bureaucracy and post-bureaucracy, it does contrast the more traditional approach at ValleyCo with the 'japanized' approach at Nippon CTV where there is a focus on lean production, just-in-time management, innovation, customer focus and HRM – all the paraphernalia of the post-bureaucratic workplace.

Whilst Delbridge found a number of contrasts between the plants, it is fair to say that his overall conclusion is that there is a considerable similarity between 'traditional' and 'new' forms of working in terms of things like hierarchy, participation or trust:

> There is little to suggest that contemporary manufacturing is best characterised as 'postfordist' and that the shop-floor is a hotbed of worker autonomy and knowledge creation. (Delbridge, 1998: 192)

These kinds of studies might seem like the best way of countering the claims of post-bureaucracy's flagwavers. They certainly act as an antidote to the extravagant and self-serving claims such as those contained within Ricardo Semler's (1993) account of his firm Semco, a Brazilian engineering firm. Semler regards himself as a 'counsellor' rather than a chief executive, and this illustrates the idea that post-bureaucracy discounts hierarchy. Overall, Semco is characterized by an approach which rejects formal rules, where employees set their own working hours and pay rates and which is relaxed about unionization and strike activity. But this account downplays the way that the 'new' Semco was predicated upon wholesale redundancies in the old corporation. These are mentioned, but as necessary blows against bureaucratic inertia and without any attention to what the experiences of the downsized bureaucrats might be (did they starve to death? We don't know and, in Semler's narrative, are given no reason to care). More importantly, unlike studies such as that of Delbridge, we hear nothing at all of the voice and experience of those who actually work there. We are simply invited to take on trust the organization as refracted through Semler's lens.

Is, say, Thompson right? Is Semler wrong? These are endlessly contestable questions. The adequacy of evidence selected and the adequacy of the way it is interpreted are crucial; but this adequacy will be assessed in the light of pre-existing prejudices, arguments and views. So, for all their virtues, I wonder if empirical refutations of the post-bureaucracy thesis are enough. They help, of course, but they rest on a perhaps naïve assumption that the facts will, or can, speak for themselves. Unfortunately, that does not really meet the cunning of the opposition. They will respond that the kinds of developments discussed by the critics are 'not really' post-bureaucracy and that, in any case, whilst instances of post-bureaucracy may be thin on the ground they are, nonetheless, the future of organizations. They will find particular examples that conform to the case, and these examples may be well-founded. If pushed, they may even say that for all that the world is not so very post-bureaucratic, it would be better if it were.

So what is needed (alongside empirical counter-examples) is a way of questioning the very structure, presumptions and assumptions of the post-bureaucratic argument. Shift the terms of debate and you shift the filter through which any evidence is evaluated. Apart from mocking its presumptuousness and questioning its evidence, a third way of doing this is to question the desirability of the post-bureaucratic model as an ideal – whether or not it exists. An example is Paul du Gay's (2000) argument about bureaucracy, mentioned in Chapter 1. Here, the case was made that bureaucracy, for all its critics, embodies an ethic of fairness which is bound up with impersonal treatment. Critics may complain that it dehumanizes, but they miss the protections this offers.

Heckscher's post-bureaucracy points up very sharply what is at stake here. Post-bureaucracy does away with the turgid old nonsense about impersonality, yearly promotions and fixed salary scales in favour of individual treatment where reward is based on merit. How refreshing; for which of us wishes to be treated as anything other than an individual? Which of us wishes to get the same pay rise, after all the work we have done, as the time-serving hack at the next desk? Fine. So, now, how is our pay rise going to be determined? By performance? But who will judge this performance? Perhaps – as with the case for and against post-bureaucracy – the facts will speak for themselves. The difficulty is that there is an endless range of contextual factors to individual performance that any assessor may (and very likely will) be unable to determine. Personal treatment means treatment at whim. It may be overtly corrupt – those with pretty faces get the best deal. It may just depend upon the sincerely held judgments of our assessors. Either way, our desire to be treated individually can conflict sharply with our desire to be treated fairly. And suddenly, post-bureaucracy recedes as a utopian ideal and comes into focus as potentially a site of prejudice and incompetence.

why are you always carping?

If you have followed the argument so far but are unpersuaded by it, then you may well be thinking something along these lines: will nothing ever satisfy you? Older approaches to organizations have been condemned as dehumanizing and degrading. Human relations-type approaches are manipulative. Culture management is brainwashing.

Now we have non-hierarchical, personally focussed and trust-based organizations and you are still whinging. Your sort make me sick.

This is a good, *Daily Mail*[1]-type reaction. It's a strange thing, though. People who are impatient with those who criticize organizations are often the same people who react with horror to the impredations of governmental bureaucracy. Leave us alone to be individuals, without any politically correct interference from 'so-called intellectuals'. So isn't it strange that the nostrums of those who by any standard deserve the derogatory label 'so-called intellectual' are so readily accepted, and the erosion of individuality they propose is so little opposed? The key here is to understand the incoherence of the arguments proposed within the 'war on bureaucracy'.

Consider education. In a high-profile case in 2000, Oxford University applicant Laura Spence was rejected for an over-subscribed medicine course despite having 3 A-grade A-levels (the fact that many Oxbridge applicants have 5 As was forgotten). A state school applicant (albeit from a middle-class background), it was alleged that she had been discriminated against by a procedure that included an individual interview. How does this relate to bureaucracy and post-bureaucracy? If selection had focussed only on formal qualifications then it would be bureaucratic, and thus criticizable on the grounds of failing to take individual circumstances into account. The interview process did take these circumstances into account, but was dismissed as elitist.

It was bemoaned as unfair that she had 'lost out' (in quarters that were horrified by the 'politically correct' rejection of competition in schools). The suggestion was that her state school background had made her the victim of bias (in quarters that defended the right of parents to buy a superior education for their children). But when Bristol University subsequently introduced a system to discriminate in favour of state school applicants by looking at their results in the context of the school they came from, which is to say a post-bureaucratic system to take account of individual circumstances, this

---

1   For the benefit of non-UK readers, the *Daily Mail* is a popular British newspaper which attacks anything it perceives as violating an imagined norm of suburban decency. 'Bogus' asylum seekers (and foreigners in general), intellectuals (especially 'so-called'), artists (especially 'modern'), 'metropolitans', 'cosmopolitans', feminists, liberals etc. are all regarded as hate figures.

was seen as 'political correctness gone mad' and outrageous 'social engineering'. University places, said such commentators, should be allocated on exam achievement, which is to say, by a bureaucratic system.

What the university admissions issue (which continues to rattle on, years after the Laura Spence case) shows is the endless contestability of the debate over bureaucracy and post-bureaucracy. These are most obvious in relation to public sector organizations, for it is these which capture political and public attention. To take some examples, in health there is a constant complaint about the bureaucratic targets set by meddling civil servants. Let individual hospitals determine what is best without the dead hand of bureaucracy. But when they do, inevitably differences arise between different areas. This is then depicted as the scandal of the 'postcode lottery', to which the solution can only be – centrally determined bureaucratic targets. Or in schools, where the accusation in the 1980s was that these were adopting all manner of dogmas, with sex education undermining responsible family life; history being taught in terms of capitalist and colonialist repression; even sport being denuded of the competitive ethic. The solution was to introduce centralized, bureaucratic methods of quality assurance and the prescription of a national curriculum. Roll forward to today and the complaint is that we have a restrictive, bureaucratic and centralized administration and the solution is to devolve power to school level. It doesn't take a genius to predict that if this solution is implemented then, in a few years time, there will be calls for centralized control to prevent the 'abuses' of local freedom. At its most generic, the issue is that if systemic rules treat individuals badly then the call is for more discrimination for individuals, but if individual treatment results in bad outcomes then the call is for more rule-based systems.

This dilemma serves to point up some important issues (including how politics can deal with so contradictory set of demands). One is that the design of organizations, whether in the public sector or not, is not some neutral, 'technical' issue in the way that managerial approaches to organization fantasize is the case. Assuming that – as is usually the case – the outputs of organizations matter to people, the way that they are organized must be the subject of different views and interests and therefore is necessarily in the domain of values and not just techniques. Second, these examples show that those who

confidently propound a post-bureaucratic future display an ignorance about the very reasons why bureaucratic organizations
emerged. This is not to say that such organizations are particularly
praiseworthy. In Chapter 1, I outlined the various kinds of 'bureaucratic dysfunctionalism' that are part of what constitutes the case
against bureaucracy. But there is also a post-bureaucratic dysfunctionalism, in which fairness, consistency and transparency are
absent, which should be considered alongside any advantages the
'new model' may have. Perhaps more than anything else, bureaucracy with its procedures, its stifling routine, is said to prevent innovation, risk-taking and entrepreneurial zeal. This may be true, but it
also protects us from the risks of ill-considered innovation and if it
should come to be that the future is post-bureaucratic it may well
also be a future where spectacular failures occur; and if it is true that
the outputs of organizations matter to people, then they may come
to rue the day when risk was embraced with such recklessness.

The strongest moral case for post-bureaucracy is, of course, that
it addresses the dehumanization associated with bureaucracy. This is
not a new claim, since it was also made for human relations
approaches within traditional organizations. And as with those
claims it founders on the grounds which I guess I have rehearsed ad
nauseam already. Bureaucracy does dehumanize to the extent that it
reduces its employees (and customers) to the level of cogs in the
organizational machine. But the humanization offered by post-
bureaucracy, like that found in culture management, offers only a
truncated version of humanity – the freedom to align oneself with
the organizational machine. The fact that the former tries to suppress human agency whilst the latter tries to harness it is scarcely a
compelling difference.

A moment ago, I referred to post-bureaucracy as a 'new model'.
Why the speechmarks? Because all this talk of a new era and new
organizational forms conceals or forgets the way that such claims are
recurring so that it is possible to find, throughout organization theory,
almost identical models of the future. To understand this amnesia, it is
necessary to address what is probably the most fundamental aspect of
contemporary approaches to studying organizations. If the most
fundamental part of the classical approaches was the modernist
assumption of manageability, its counterpart in contemporary
approaches is the 'postmodernist' preoccupation with 'change'. Or,
more accurately, the way that these two fundamentals are combined in
the sine qua non of contemporary approaches – change management.

▰▰▰▰ this changing world

What ties together almost all of the issues about culture management, post-bureaucracy and the contemporary preoccupations of mainstream organization theory is, I think, the centrality placed upon the concept of change. Change provides a kind of 'meta-narrative', an overarching rationale or assumption which then acts as an explicit or implicit justification for specific change programmes in organizations. So ubiquitous is the invocation of change, and so crucial is it to the claims which follow from it, that it seems reasonable to describe it as a fetish. Grint (1997: 35) refers to the fetish for change in an analysis of management fashions and fads, but its significance goes beyond these. Change is a notion which is drawn upon in a largely unthinking, but very significant, way so that it takes on an almost magical character. Change is like a totem before which we must prostrate ourselves and in the face of which we are powerless.

Perhaps the most interesting feature of the change fetish is the way in which it figures as the contextual, introductory and taken for granted. So obvious is it taken to be that it typically takes the form of rushed assertions at the outset of any particular treatment of organizations and management. For example:

> In a changing world the only constant is change ... the reality is that the stability which seemed to characterise the corporate world in the 1950s and 1960s has given way to increased and global competition, technological innovation and change, limited resources, deregulation, privatisation of public sector organizations and change in much more besides. (Carnall, 1995: 1)

Open just about any book on organization theory or management written in the last 20 years and, in one form or another, you will find a similar formulation – almost always on the introductory page.[2] This is partly because many of these texts feed off each other: referencing

---

2 As I implied earlier, these claims recur, always believing themselves to be new. Thus Parker et al. comment that '[t]wo accepted clichés about contemporary societies are that they are experiencing unprecedented rates of change and that they have been drawn together by trade and mass communications into a global village' (1977: 172). Jacques (1996) notes how many of the claims about a second industrial revolution in the late twentieth century are almost identical to those made in the early part of the century. Yet those earlier periods are recast as being stable in later accounts.

each other, drawing ideas off each other, looking to each other for supporting evidence. This does not invalidate them, for all discursive formations exhibit this kind of interlocking structure, but it does create a remarkably unchallenged consensus about the 'fact' of change.

And it is not just within organization theory that notions of unprecedented change are invoked. What really marks out the power of the change fetish is the way that it figures in just about every magazine and newspaper article about business as a background assumption, as well as in training courses and seminars. Whenever I meet managers – or management students, for that matter – I find that, almost without exception, they produce the same mantra: the world is changing at an ever-faster rate and organizations must change in line with it. There have been – recently – a few texts questioning facets of the fetish of change, but only a very few. Certainly, at least for the time being, such questioning is not reflected in the wider literature, still less in popular management texts.

Of course, to describe a world in change might be no more than a rather self-evident comment about the character of human existence. Heraclites of Ephesus, the Ancient Greek philosopher, suggested that all things are in flux, albeit at different rates, famously pointing out that when you put your foot in a river it immediately ceases to be the same river. Simply by virtue of being in time, change is occurring. But the fetish of change goes much beyond this. First, it conceptualizes current rates of change as unprecedented. Second, it ascribes change not to the ineluctable character of time but to certain determinate features, such as technology and globalization. Third, change is envisaged as something amenable to interventions rather than as a spontaneous flux.

The notion of managing change typically refers not to attempts to manage the wider changes of the economy and technology but to attempts to manage organizational responses (whether 'reactive' or 'proactive') to these. In other words, change management refers to attempts by organizations to change themselves in response to actual or predicted environmental change. And such responses are not thought of as being optional: organizations which do not respond adequately to environmental change will not survive in the face of, in particular, competition.

Of course the judgments about what *types* of change must be made in organizations and the methods of achieving these changes will vary according to situation. In some cases it will be a matter of developing new products, or marketing existing products in a new way. In other cases it will be investment in new technologies; vertical or horizontal integrations; geographical relocations or any number of other things. Despite this diversity, one of the common themes of organizational change in recent years has been changes in organizational design associated with culture management and the assault on bureaucracy.

It is unlikely that there is anyone who has spent any time at all studying organizations or, for that matter, working in them in recent years who has not been exposed to the assumption that change is getting more rapid and is vital to organizational survival. This, I suggest, has become a central part of the common-sense and taken-for-granted knowledge about organizations.

reasons for scepticism

I want now to suggest that there are a number of reasons to be sceptical about common sense in relation to change and change management.

The first issue is that the belief that we live in times of unprecedented change is one which is found in many ages, and perhaps every age. In retrospect the past seems more stable than the present because it is familiar to us and because we experience it in the sanitized and rationalized form of history books or through the haze of nostalgic memory. Yet it is possible to point to any number of periods in the past when, for those alive, it must have seemed as if the world was changing in unprecedented and dramatic ways: the collapse of the Roman Empire; the colonization of the Americas; the Renaissance; the Reformation; the Enlightenment; the Industrial Revolution; the World Wars. The shift from religious to secular conceptions of the world over the last four centuries has, and continues to have, massive ramifications throughout the world, beside which any issues of globalization and technical change experienced in recent years, even accepting these at face value, seem fairly limited.

There is no reason to think that the present time is one of greater change than in the past, nor that we are the first people to experience change as being unprecedented. Or, to put it differently, and perhaps rather better, there is no *basis* upon which it would be possible to sustain or evaluate such claims. Who is to say that the changes associated with the microchip are faster or more far-reaching than those associated with the printing press? What dimensions of change are we talking about? For whom? Is it possible to attribute causation to particular technologies anyway, given that these are part of a network of social relations which are part and parcel of the inventions and discoveries to which they give rise?

What we do know is that there is a tendency to look back to the past as a 'golden age' now lost by the travails of time. For example, it's familiar how fears about crime show a recurring pattern of beliefs that '20 years ago' we lived in a period of stability, order and morality. In terms of organization theory there seems to be, as I said earlier, a belief that there has been a fundamental shift from the 'good old days' of stable bureaucracies, mass markets, Fordism and modernism to the new world of post-bureaucracy, niche markets, post-Fordism and postmodernism. The authorized version of organization theory normally periodizes this in terms of a stable era from 1945 through to the oil crisis of 1974.

Yet in many respects one would hardly classify the post-war order as one of stability, whether economically, politically or technologically. The received wisdom of post-war stability rather conveniently ignores, inter alia, the space race; development of computers; the Cold War; the arms race; de-colonization; the Korean and Vietnam wars; the feminist movement; major waves of immigration and emigration; major shifts in youth culture and the relations between generations. It is not clear that these constituted a 'stable environment'.

Let me shift the analysis for a moment from the general to the personal – and these are by no means separate realms, for the one invariably constitutes the other. In 1945 my late father was an agricultural labourer in Britain. By 1948 he had travelled thousands of miles to work in large-scale mechanized agriculture in Canada. In 1952 he was up to his neck in mud fixing tanks in Korea. Around the same time, my late father-in-law was fleeing the Bulgarian secret police hanging beneath the Orient Express from Sofia in mid-winter. After various periods as a prisoner in Tito's Yugoslavia and international camps, he escaped to France, an illegal immigrant with no money, no friends and barely any clothes. I don't think that either of these men would recognize the picture of post-war stability found in the textbooks.

Even the jewel in the crown of the change fetish – increased globalization – is by no means as clear-cut an issue as is commonly supposed. Hirst and Thompson's important (1996) book exposes claims about economic globalization to rigorous and sceptical scrutiny. Comparing the ratio of trade to gross domestic product (GDP), for example, they find that this has dropped in most industrialized countries over the course of the twentieth century, and using a range of measures they claim that 'unequivocally ... openness was more in the Gold Standard period than even in the 1980s' (Hirst and Thompson, 1996: 28). With slightly less confidence, they argue that migration (of people) was substantially less in the twentieth century than the nineteenth, certainly as a proportion of the world's population. Overall, they conclude that 'the international economy was hardly less integrated before 1914 than it is today' (1996: 196–7).

None of this is to say that change does not occur. However, what is at issue is how change is apprehended within particular cultural and historical settings. The key point is that if – as is the case in mainstream contemporary organization theory – we collectively construe our times as being characterized by rapid and unprecedented change, then we are likely, through acting on that belief, to render it self-fulfilling, so that this construction is real in its effects – effects which are discussed in the next chapter. It is necessary, then, to understand the perspectival nature of change: what matters is how we see it, and that depends on where we look from.

the treadmill of change

Organization theory typically looks from, or through, a number of metaphors which have the effect of legitimating the fetish of change. Perhaps the most longstanding is the mechanistic metaphor of the organization as machine. This, in line with the classical approaches I discussed earlier in this book, licenses a vision of the change manager as an engineer. But in terms of the *justification* of change, the more important metaphor is organismic. This stresses, first, the idea of the organization as distinct from the environment and, second, the necessity of adaptation of the former to the latter.

Such debates leave untouched the fundamental assumption of a boundary between the inside and outside of an organization (a boundary which also allows most organization theory to ignore society, culture, history and philosophy). But where is this boundary? Is it that of the physical premises of an organization? Plainly not, because, for example, networks of supply and distribution affect and are affected by the organization whilst lying outside its physical boundaries. Is it the people employed? Plainly not, because what about customers, shareholders and so on? Insofar as any boundaries can be discerned between an organization and its environment, these are defined through socially and historically specific conventions.

More specifically, organizational boundaries are defined through the deployment of certain bodies of expertise such as law or accounting. Yet these are conventions or constructs. An organization may be able, legally, to regard the locality and community around it as external so that the social costs of laying off workers or polluting the environment (in the ecological sense) are not borne by the organization. However, there is no necessity in this line – it is not 'natural' – since companies could be made to account for externalities and held liable for various effects.

As well as conceiving of organizations as distinct from their environments, common sense, backed up by conventional organizational theory, configures the relationship between the two as a Darwinian one in which those which adapt to the environment survive whilst those which do not are doomed. The Darwinian metaphor is perhaps particularly associated with the population–ecology model of organizations (Aldrich, 1979), although it has come to be used far more widely, and imprecisely, as part of the general vocabulary of management. Interestingly, the strict interpretation of the population–ecology model would suggest there is no scope for management to influence the success or failure of an organization's fit with the environment, and hence its survival, since the environment 'selects' organizations. However, the more general impact of structural contingency and strategic choice theory suggests that a 'fit' between organizations and their environments is something that can be, and is, achieved managerially. Certainly the latter is the *core* assumption of all change management ideas which are necessarily predicated upon the belief that organizations can be managed in ways that 'make a difference' to the capacity of an organization to succeed in its environment.

But I am anticipating what will be discussed more fully later. Returning to organismic metaphors, these are unhelpful because they conceal the sense in which organizations and environments are mutually constitutive. Plainly, the environment of any organization (call it organization A) consists of other organizations, and each of those organizations operates in an environment of which organization A is a part. Organization A is therefore not just part of the environment of *other* organizations, but also part of its *own* environment. This is not to be confused with the proposition that organizations and environments are interdependent: rather it is to say that positing the very notions of organization and environment as separate is misleading.

In less abstract terms, this means that as an organization changes, it contributes to the rationale for change in other organizations, which in turn provide a rationale for change in the original organization. Ultimately this is likely to be futile: suppose an organization implements, for example, total quality management (TQM) for 'the first time in the world' (or for the first time in a particular industry) and further suppose that this yields competitive advantage. Other organizations then seek to adopt TQM and, assuming that all organizations are equally successful in their implementations, the end result will be that no organization has competitive advantage. In short, I am suggesting that organizations collectively generate a 'treadmill' of change which is then seen as a problematic environment to which an organizational response must be made.

It is indeed very obvious that TQM illustrates this point. The 'quality revolution' of the 1980s came to be seen in the 1990s as being inadequate by virtue of its attachment to 'incremental change'. A new 'revolution' was needed and instigated in the form of business process re-engineering (BPR). But BPR then became seen as 'limited' and the new vision of 'post-bureaucracy' was offered as the solution.

Of course, an obvious objection to the treadmill view I am expressing here would be to point out that, although organizations generate change collectively, any individual organization has little choice but to participate if it is to survive. It is here that the Darwinian metaphor comes into play – that survival is contingent upon adaptation because organizations that do not change will lose business to those that do. Yet there are surely reasons to doubt whether this is true. First, it cannot be assumed that organizational change does in fact lead to better or cheaper products (or to greater profitability), and, if it does not, there is no reason to assume that adaptation will be commercially beneficial. Second, even if change does lead to better or cheaper products it does not follow that customers will buy from that organization rather than another. It may be that a less good or more expensive product is compensated for by other considerations such as a particular personal relationship between buyer and seller, or habit, or convenience, or principle. To put it another way, there are all sorts of reasons why consumers are not the rational utility-maximizing agents of economic theory.

Anticipating another objection it might be thought that, currently, change programmes are often directed at giving the customer what s/he wants, including all of the 'non-rational' considerations I have just listed. However, changes conducted in the name of the customer may be very far from being the same as changes desired by the customer and may even coexist with monopoly supply of vital services, as with the privatization of some public services. Even where this is not so, many supposedly customer-oriented changes are, in reality, just the opposite. Consider the recent trend towards creating central call centres for dealing with customer enquiries in industries such as banking and insurance. Typically they involve long waits in telephone queues, dealing with elaborate automated menus and finally being connected with an automaton with no personal interest in or knowledge of the customer. In such cases, whilst change is justified in terms of the increasingly demanding nature of customers, the actual practices would seem more animated by a concern to cut costs.

In any case, the person of the customer cannot be dissociated from the person of the employee. Thus organizational change programmes which, for example, remove staff in the name of the customer and organizational survival are damaging the capacity of those staff to act as customers and, therefore, the prospects for survival of those organizations relying on this custom. This, of course, is merely another aspect of the inseparability of organizations and environments: the same individual is simultaneously a producer and a consumer.

My argument in this section is that, far from being a natural, environmental given to which organizations must respond, change is better understood as a construction affected by the interplay (and its unintended consequences) of organizations themselves. To say it is a construct is not to say that it is unreal (and I will discuss some of its effects in the next chapter), but rather that its reality is in part an effect of organizational practices rather than a precursor of those practices. Yet, by constructing a changing world, organizations also create the apparent necessity to 'manage change'. It is to this that I now turn attention.

why change management fails

The most striking thing about change management is that it almost always fails. Despite (or, who knows, because of) the reams of worthy academic treatises, the unending stream of self-congratulatory 'I did it my way' blather from pensioned-off executives and the veritable textual diarrhoea of self-serving guru handbooks, change remains a mystery. And I do not think that the answer is just around the corner: rather, change management rests upon the conceit that it is possible to systematically control social and organizational relations. But the limits to such a view are very considerable, for the reasons I have tried to explain at several points throughout this book, and will return to again in the Conclusion.

Change management a failure? Is this just wild generalization from an 'armchair critic', perhaps even a 'so-called intellectual'? But Crosby (1979) – a leading advocate of TQM – claims that 90 per cent of such projects fail to meet their targets, whilst Stewart (1993) gives a failure figure of 50–70 per cent for BPR. New techniques are announced with a great fanfare, and presented as the unproblematic solution to previous problems, but disillusion soon sets in. Some of this is bound up with the marketing activities of consultants and gurus. But there is more to it than that. Managers responsible for particular change programmes are likely, for career and identity reasons, to describe them as successful. Yet the everyday experience of people in organizations is that one change programme gives way to another in a perennially failing operation: nirvana is always just on its way.

In this context, the now massive prescriptive literature of organizational change takes on an interesting aspect. On the one hand, it must always be pointing to the failure of change management (else why the need for this new book?), whilst on the other hand, never admitting the illusory nature of successful change management (else why the need for any new book?). Much of the conflict stems here from the search for a formula or methodology which promises success in a wide variety of settings. For change management is predicated upon the substitutability of, or generalizability from, what has (supposedly) worked in one situation to another.

We can see here the social practice which underlies the observation I made earlier about the way in which organizations adopting homogeneous 'solutions' to problems in the name of competitive advantage must inevitably end up without such an advantage. For this is not just an anomaly but an inevitable feature of change management. It is most evident in relation to the very common change management methodology of 'benchmarking'. Benchmarking aims to measure and match an organization's existing products and procedures with those of competitors and, in particular, those of organizations perceived to be field leaders. It is part of a process that institutional theorists[3] have described as 'mimetic isomorphism' (DiMaggio and Powell, 1983) or, as we might more straight forwardly say, copying. Benchmarking, as a general preparation for the deployment of particular change management techniques in the name of 'best practice', is expressive of the underlying search for generalizability which characterizes change management.

According to a survey of UK Top 1000 companies, 67 per cent of such companies engage in benchmarking (cited in Carnall, 1995: 5). With an amusing circularity, the implication of this, in the context it is cited, is that since benchmarking is common in 'top' companies it should be adopted generally! Yet benchmarking embodies several obvious inanities, even within its own terms. First, there is the issue already alluded to that it can only (at best, assuming 'successful' implementation) lead to equality, not to advantage. Second, and relatedly, it might be thought that if competitive advantage is what is at stake, the thing to emulate would be the process by which an organization comes up with an original basis for innovation, rather than its outcome. Third, it seems well established that today's successful companies are very often tomorrow's failures (as mentioned earlier in this book, consider the later fate of the majority of those companies designated as 'excellent' by Peters and Waterman, 1982). Think of Enron, Arthur Andersen or Marconi. A few years ago, Marks & Spencer, the UK clothing and food retailer, was the doyen of management gurus. Then it declined and was regarded as a basket case. Then it recovered and seemed to exemplify best practice in 'turning around' a failing company. At the time of writing it is facing a decline in sales and significant loss in share price. Yet despite this there is an insatiable demand for, and invincible stupidity about, case studies and stories from such companies and a quite myopic lionization of whatever today's successes are.

But finally, and most significantly, generalizability and hence benchmarking are predicated upon the assumption that organizational settings are homogeneous with respect to the relevant features. In other words, it is assumed that doing what another organization did

---

3 One of the more interesting and influential schools within mainstream organizational theory, which does not quite fit the distinctions I drew in the introduction between positivist and constructionist, and managerialist and critical perspectives.

with a different set of people in a different place at a different time will yield the same results as those claimed for the original implementation. The irony of such an assumption is that, within a discourse obsessed with change, it relies upon everything being the same. And what do such claims amount to anyway? Let's assume an organization is successful in terms of (say) increased profitability following the intro-duction of (say) a new organizational structure. There is no way of knowing whether this success was because of, despite, or coincidental with, the new structure. It is not known, by definition, whether had another structure been adopted would the organization not have been even more profitable. There is no counterfactual, nor could there be.

Indeed, the counterfactual problem is an enduring one for change management – and management generally – irrespective of the bench-marking issue. It is never possible to know what would have happened had a change programme not been introduced, nor which effects can be assigned to which change. This problem is exacerbated by the fact that, in practice, most large organizations run several change programmes simultaneously, and typically embark upon new programmes before the old ones have 'bedded down'. All this makes both success and failure slippery concepts, and whether or not a programme is seen as successful will be an outcome of organizational politics and the context in which the outcome is being debated (for example, organizations may be happy, for public relations reasons, to figure as 'best practice' examples in management texts – the internal perception may be quite different). Finally, on this issue, what consti-tutes success is crucially, and rather obviously, dependent upon how success is defined and by whom. A successful change management programme from one perspective might be degraded and intensified work conditions from another.

Not only is it difficult – and perhaps in principle impossible – to know whether a change programme has been successful, it is also, to say the least, questionable whether change can be regarded as man-ageable at all (a parallel argument to that made in the previous chapter about culture management, which of course is one particular variant of change management). Although there are innumerable change models, the issues in this respect are well illustrated by the classic Lewin model (Lewin, 1951) still used as the basis of thinking about organizational change by many, perhaps most, consultants and managers. The basic premise of the received version of this model (I say 'received' because as with many ideas about organizations which end up as formulaic managerial knowledge, there was more complexity in the original formulation) is that there is a balance of forces which keeps a situation stable and that the task of change management is either to increase the forces for change or decrease the forces against change. Change management thus proceeds in the three steps of unfreezing, moving and refreezing.

The dominant metaphor here is mechanistic: there are 'forces' which operate to stabilize or de-stabilize an organization. The organization can be unfrozen and refrozen at will. Yet are organizations as amenable to control as (say) a block of ice? And of course this mechanistic view relates to the issue of generalizability. If the manager is a technician who understands the 'physics' of organizational force-fields and the 'mechanics' of organizational refrigeration, then plainly this implies a reliable and transferable kind of knowledge. This version of management is, of course, not unique to change but is part and parcel of the engineering model and of the top-down fantasy of managerial omnipotence found within culture management which grows out of the classical approaches to organizational theory discussed in the first part of this book.

It is worth recapping and extending what I have said so far about why this is a fantasy. It goes back to what I said in Chapter 1 about the project of management in organizations. The core issue is the inherent uncontrollability of social relations. As Roberts (1984), drawing upon the work of the philosopher Alisdair MacIntyre and the sociologist Anthony Giddens, explains, management typically assumes that systematic control of social relations is possible and therefore treats people as if they are simply objects rather than also as subjects. In other words, people are assumed to be passive receivers of others' actions rather than being themselves actors who can (and do) respond differentially to events, interpret them in a differential way and deliberately or unwittingly obstruct and subvert these actions. People are capable of noticing and reflecting upon what goes on around them, and of acting differently, for whatever reason, as a result.

The capacity (and necessity) of people to be both subjects and objects links much of what I have said both in this chapter and throughout this book. It explains why mechanistic understandings of change (and management generally) are so inappropriate. For all the talk of forces and freezing, people do not act in the same way as molecules of water: they act in ways that are both unpredictable but, more importantly, which are subject to deliberate and intentional change on the part of the individuals concerned. By the same token, mechanistic understandings underlie the issues of generalizability and the counterfactual problem. If the issue were simply one of freezing and refreezing molecules of water it would be possible to say that given like conditions, which could readily be replicated, the molecules will behave in the same way. But in organizations like conditions can never – literally never – be specified or replicated.

None of this should be reduced to the trite observation that the problem for change management is that 'people are all individuals'. What is at stake here is that people exist within a range of meaning structures (including those, discussed in Chapter 2, that allow people to experience their agency as an individual attribute) of which the organizational is only one. These meaning structures are indeterminate and open-ended, and therefore unpredictable in their effects and likely to give rise to unintended consequences.

In this sense, the problems encountered by change management are an aspect of the problems of social science in general. Indeed, much organization theory derives from social science, albeit often in bowdlerized form. Yet, as mentioned earlier, the promise of control derived from social science is illusory. So it should not be thought, as some diehards claim, that going back to social science (even in some more rigorous way than managers have been wont to do) to get better models will solve the problem of control since, in this respect, social sciences are 'almost or perhaps completely devoid of achievement. For the salient fact about these sciences is the absence of any law-like generalisations whatsoever' (MacIntyre, 1981: 88).

conclusion

Organization theory may be said to have started with an observation, by Max Weber no less, that the modern world had broken with the past in its preoccupation with the technical efficiency provided by bureaucracy. That observation still seems, with a great deal of hindsight, to be very well founded. Ever since then, there have been endless proclamations of another new era, but these do not seem to be so well founded. I think the post-bureaucracy claim is a case in point. Now of course this kind of thing is difficult to judge. 'History never looks like history when you are living through it. It always looks confusing and messy and it always feels uncomfortable' said John Gardner (in Daintith, 2000: 81). So I may be wrong (but, for the same reasons, the proponents of post-bureaucracy should be wary).

Predictably, I don't think I am wrong, though. I have referred to some empirical evidence that calls the post-bureaucracy thesis into question. However, to be fair, I have also indicated that this kind of argument isn't likely to be settled by empirical evidence given the problems of interpretation. But what may be more important is that I have, I hope, showed that whatever the empirics of organizations, in terms of organization theory there is a very strong continuity which seems to give the lie to this new-era thinking.

For what is striking is not just the repetition of the claims about new organizational forms and the management of change which will bring them into existence, but the repetition of a way of thinking that shows almost no development from the classical approaches to organization theory that I outlined in the first two chapters. For all the talk about new paradigms, contemporary organization theory and managerial method remain remarkably unchanged from their classical roots. Not just because techniques like benchmarking[4] are, a hundred years after Taylor, still to the fore but more importantly because the underlying philosophy of instrumental rationality and control remains firmly in the ascendant. This means that the post-bureaucratic revolution is extremely unlikely to succeed, but it also means that, even if it were to succeed, it would only initiate an even more intensive and even less morally defensible subjugation of human potentiality.

Does this mean that all this talk of post-bureaucracy and change can just be ignored? Unfortunately not. For there can be no doubt that they have exerted a considerable hold over the managerial imagination. In organizations, the kind of organization theory I have discussed in this chapter enjoys a remarkable ascendancy and this is most obvious, because it attracts most media attention, in public sector organizations. At least in the UK, almost every government policy is predicated on the assumptions of post-bureaucracy, sometimes explicitly using this term and almost invariably invoking the mantra of change. It is assumed that public services must be purged of bureaucracy and that the economy must change to be able to compete in a globalized knowledge economy. And it is assumed that what matters in policy is 'what works' – in other words, the instrumental rationality of organization theory has been taken up as a political philosophy. Once again, the boundary between organization theory

---

4   The very word 'benchmarking' is, literally, an engineering term.

and other arenas is a fuzzy one, but in this case, rather than import political issues into organization theory, politics has adopted the dubious nostrums of managerial versions of organization theory.

In doing so, I believe that politicians have used organization theory in precisely the way that, in the Introduction to this book, I claimed that theory is always used: as a way of pursuing particular agendas. All these claims about post-bureaucracy and change are really an exercise of power. Anyone who questions them is automatically painted as retrograde, old-fashioned, elitist, resistant to change and, fundamentally, out of step with the modern world. Change is a crass theology, but a theology it is. It is the doctrinal orthodoxy of those who rule us. Be insufficiently worshipful of its doctrine and you will be punished. Inflexibility, 'irrational' resistance to change, lack of entrepreneurial zeal: these are the new heresies. But bemoan it as I may, its effects are real enough, and it is these which I explore in the next chapter.

5

Fast Capitalism and the
End of Management

Instant gratification takes too long.
Carrie Fisher

I indicated in the previous chapter that we need to be very wary of the extravagant, generalized claims of those who proclaim a new and unprecedented era of change within which organizations exist and to which they must respond. Such 'epochal thinking' (du Gay, 2003) with its 'cartoon concepts' (Froud et al., 2006: 66) such as post-bureaucracy is at best over-simplified and at worst acts to justify punitive assaults on people's lives and livelihoods. However, it would be equally flawed to claim that, somehow, nothing changes or has changed and to fail to understand organizations within their wider cultural and economic context.

In this chapter I want, to a greater extent than I have before, to locate the study of organizations within this wider context. Of course to do this fully would require much more space than I can devote to it – several long books, in fact – so I am going to concentrate on some contemporary issues about the kind of society and economy that has emerged over recent decades in the West, and more particularly on the idea that this society and economy are characterized by a preoccupation with speed. Apart from introducing these issues, I also want to underscore what has been a major theme of this book: that when we study organizations we must necessarily be concerned with politics, economics, history and society. For reasons that I will discuss in the next chapter, it is a major failing of most courses on organizations that they, and knowledge about them, are presented in a way which is denuded of such things, except perhaps in the form of a few trite claims and unstated assumptions about them. But that failing is part and parcel of treating the study of organizations as a 'technical' matter of delivery, rather than probing the question of what is delivered and why.

So what sort of world do contemporary organizations inhabit and create? According to a wide range of commentators, we now live within 'liquid modernity' (Bauman, 2000) or 'hypermodernity' (Virilio, 1977). Paul Virilio also coined the term 'dromology' to denote the analysis of the compulsive logic of speed within hypermodernity. The anthropologist Philip Augé (1995) argues that this implies a 'supermodernity' in which cultural life has speeded up to the extent that the frame of history has changed, with the very recent past becoming immediately a subject for historical reflection and the present being immediately evaluated for its historicity. For example, even before Tony Blair stepped down as the UK's Prime Minister in 2007 there were lengthy TV 'retrospectives' of his time in office and assessments of his historical standing and legacy. In early 2008 a play, 'The Death of Margaret Thatcher', opened in London even though Thatcher herself is still alive. Very recent events, even current events, have become the subject of 'factional' dramas and the music and films of the immediate past become packaged up for nostalgic viewing by digital TV channels. These are particular instances of Harvey's (1989) notion of time–space compression in which traditional conceptions of distance and speed have been dramatically telescoped (for example, by global communications). Coming back to organizations, it is also consistent with Richard Sennett's (2006: 127) observation that within the 'new capitalism' corporations are almost completely uninterested in the past, but instead value only present, and more importantly future, achievements.

Again, and despite the language of these kinds of analyses, we shouldn't envisage the speeding up of life as indicative of a 'new epoch'. In fact, a preoccupation with speed and transformation is all of a piece with modernity and capitalism. As long ago as 1848, those poor old 'lefties' Marx and Engels observed in *The Communist Party Manifesto* that:

> The bourgeoisie cannot exist without constantly revolutionizing the instruments of production and thereby the relations of production, and with them the whole relations of society. Conservation of the old modes of production in unaltered form was, on the contrary, the first condition of existence for all earlier industrial classes. Constant revolutionizing of production, uninterrupted disturbance of all social conditions, everlasting uncertainty and agitation distinguish the bourgeois epoch from all earlier ones. All fixed fast-frozen relations, with their train of ancient and venerable prejudices and opinions, are swept away, all new-formed ones become antiquated before they can ossify.

All that is solid melts into air, all that is holy is profaned, and man is at last compelled to face with sober senses his real conditions of life and his relations with his kind. (Marx and Engels in Freedman, 1962: 14)

And not only is this not a new thing, but also it isn't just about capitalism. Rather it is to do with the way that western society has proceeded since the scientific revolution of the seventeenth century initiated the Modern era. As the now rather neglected writer Lewis Mumford expressed it:

Power, speed, motion, standardization, mass production, quantification, regimentation, precision, uniformity, astronomical regularity, control, above all control – these became the passwords of modern society in the new Western style. (Mumford, 1967: 294)

What is at stake, then, in speeding up is the intensification of pre-existing characteristics of western capitalism, rather than a wholesale rupture with the past. What does this mean for organizations?

fast and footloose capitalism

Until relatively recently, organizations often retained an identifiable link with places and communities. This was reflected in their names. Banks and building societies were, in the UK, called things like the Midland or the Halifax. Airlines were national flag carriers for their countries, and were normally nationally owned. And company names reflected not just place but function: they were gas firms or water firms, for example. That naming has either changed or become meaningless. Thus Midland is subsumed into HSBC, Halifax into HBOS. Abbey National became Abbey and is owned by the huge Spanish financial conglomerate Santander. Airline ownership is largely dispersed: they now rarely have a connection with the country they reference, or have names which don't reference a country at all (Virgin, EasyJet, etc.). Thames Water and Yorkshire Power belong to a German company, RWE; British Airports Authority belongs to the Spanish firm Ferovial; British Gas is owned by Centrica.[1] British names such as HP

---

1   It is part and parcel of the phenomenon I am describing that by the time you read this the details are likely to have changed, but the general outline remains the same.

sauce, Beefeater Gin, P&O, Weetabix, Jaguar, Rolls-Royce, Hamley's, OXO, Body Shop, Bass beer, even Harry Ramsden's Fish and Chips shops – and hundreds of others – are now owned by international companies or consortia. Those interested in football (personally I've never been able to get into it) might wish to consider the way that football clubs – at least the elite clubs like Manchester United and Chelsea – now have little connection either in their ownership, their players or their fan base with the localities to which their names bear testament. Indeed, at the time of writing, there is a proposal that English Premier League matches might be played at a variety of international locations in order to maximize revenue.

This isn't a nostalgic, nationalistic lament, even if to my students I may increasingly appear to be a grumpy old man (I prefer the term 'seasoned'). Nor is it parochialism. Rather, I use these examples because Britain has been especially willing to see its companies sold off[2] and this is because, in a sense, just as Britain was in the vanguard of the industrial revolution, so too – along with, in particular, the US and New Zealand – was it one of the first developed economies to embrace the neo-liberal revolution of the 1980s and has been a 'first mover' in the subsequent advent of fast and footloose capitalism.[3]

The relaxed attitude to the internationalization of ownership of what were once UK companies reflects a distinctive attitude to organizations. Understood as 'brands', ownership doesn't really matter – indeed, many of the brands I have alluded to continue to exist, even though their ownership has changed. But understood as the products of organizations, it most certainly does. The link between ownership, work and community is a complex one, which the language of brands fails to understand. A localized employer, rooted in an area with a workforce that has long-standing personal and familial ties with that product and that employer, is an important source of community. Once the link is broken, then not only are

---

2 Successive French governments, to take an obvious contrast with the UK case, including the present regime, have consistently acted to avoid such sell-offs, especially as regards strategically important industries, for example blocking foreign takeovers of energy and banking firms. Another interesting contrast is the outrage in the US when in 2006 a UK company, P&O, sold off its interests in US ports to a United Arab Emirates company. Such outrage is almost entirely absent in the UK.

3 It is an irony that would repay considerable analysis that although the UK has wholeheartedly embraced the international mobility of capital, it continues to agonize over the internationalization of politics, in the form of the European Union, and the international mobility of labour in the form of immigration.

workplace practices likely to change but so too is the meaning of work itself. So too is the meaning of ownership: why should a dispersed, international ownership 'care' about a business above and beyond its financial value? So too is the relationship between business and politics: can individual governments regulate such organizations or must they rather compete to attract them?

Of course there have always been takeovers and mergers of companies, but what is happening now is that companies are traded and re-traded endlessly so that there is never a moment of stability in which ownership patterns settle down. There is an endless re-shuffling of the corporate card deck, as if the players of a game of Monopoly were not only suffering from attention deficit disorder but were also taking amphetamines. And remember that what is being traded isn't cards, it isn't even brands – it is the lives and livelihoods of the people who work for these companies. These are the chips being played with in what the late Susan Strange evocatively described as the 'casino capitalism' which emerged from the whole-sale deregulation of financial markets in the 1980s (Strange, 1986).

The transformation of the corporate landscape to one of free-wheeling globalized financial deals is part and parcel of what the Australian writers Gee et al. (1996) persuasively call the 'fast capitalist story' in which constant transformation of organizations, and constant speeding up of work within those organizations, is mandatory to organizational survival in ways that clearly echo my discussion of post-bureaucracy and change in Chapter 4. In calling it a 'story' they do not mean that it is untrue, but rather that it is an ideology with real effects: that is, to the extent that the story is accepted and acted upon, then the consequences will be real for organizations and individuals who are not 'fast enough', and they will be *punitive*. Gee et al.'s analysis is consistent with a rash of related observations made by several influential commentators on the nature of contemporary society and capitalism, including those referred to at the outset of this chapter as well as Edward Luttwak (1999), who popularized the now widely used term 'turbocapitalism' to denote these developments, and Boltanski and Chiapello's (2007) analysis of 'the new spirit of capitalism'. Whilst all of the works I have referred to are nuanced in different ways, use different termi-nologies and have different modes of explanation, they are all, I think, circling a similar set of issues to that of fast capitalism.

It is within the context of the fast capitalist story that we should understand the notion of a supposed rupture between 'old' and 'new' capitalisms, of the sort criticized in Chapter 4. Nigel Thrift (2005) points to the ways in which twenty-first century capitalism has become ever-more preoccupied with, and sophisticated in, giving accounts of itself. In this sense capitalism has, for Thrift, become 'knowing capitalism' in that it is not simply the subject of analysis by social scientists and political commentators but through, for example, management gurus, academics and the business press, provides an ongoing commentary upon *itself*. This social 'reflexivity' is distinctive if not in its nature then at least in its intensity and proliferation, and central to it is an account of capitalism that stresses a new era of speed, change, flexibility and agility. This account is highly self-serving because whilst purporting to be *descriptive* it acts as a *prescription* for an ever-greater speeding up of, and therefore a rootless and anarchic approach to, organization. And whilst, as we have seen, this is not 'new', the extent to which invocations of fast capitalism are widespread and ideologically potent and therefore real in their effects has become increasingly important.

Sennett (2006: 37–41), in his discussion of 'the new capitalism', locates these and similar developments in the unleashing of huge amounts of investment capital following the collapse of the Bretton Woods agreement (the system which had regulated international trade and currency movements since the end of the Second World War) in the 1970s. This in turn led to a period of massive restructuring through mergers and acquisitions. Stability, indeed, became seen as a sign of weakness and companies had 'to look beautiful in the eyes of the passing voyeur [by] demonstrating signs of internal change and flexibility' (Sennett, 2006: 40). One might say that the display of this beauty became one of the 'symbols' of the economy of disorganized capitalism identified by Lash and Urry (1994). Such a capitalism is no longer primarily concerned with the production of useful goods and services, but is rather about the promulgation of brands and the pursuit of 'value'. More specifically, the value sought within the new capitalism has in recent decades been increasingly accented towards the narrow goal of the maximization of 'shareholder value', a process described as 'financialization' (Froud et al., 2006).[4]

---

4   But there are wider definitions of financialization. It is not just about the prioriti-
     zation of shareholder value, but about the idea that firms are not primarily about
     the delivery of goods and services so much as vehicles for financial engineering. It
     is this understanding of the corporation which primarily informs 'fast capitalism'.

In the last few years one of the fastest growing 'industries' in the Developed World is that of private equity. Its growth is intimately connected with the shifting corporate landscape described earlier. Private equity firms specialize in buying up companies, normally using borrowed money, and subjecting them to drastic reorganizations, usually involving large-scale redundancies and work intensification, designed to generate very rapid returns before selling the companies off to new owners. To critics, this amounts to asset stripping – simply squeezing money out of a business with no thought to long-term considerations, to customers or to employers. Whether or not this is the case, what is more to the point is that private equity firm activity represents no more than the latest, if perhaps most intensive, phase in the ratcheting up of the speed of organizational life. This ratcheting up is explored in an innovative way by Hancock (2006) who studied a range of organizational documents, and in particular visual images. These range from the explicit lionization of speed as a central aspect of business, for example the delivery firm Fedex which boasts that 'everything happens at breakneck speed' (2006: 632), to the more subtle invocation of 'vitality', for example in the case of global professional services firm PWC. These kinds of images embody what Hancock, with a nod towards the words of Marx and Engels quoted earlier in this chapter, calls the 'glorification of the world of melting solids' (2006: 631).

This glorification is an important aspect of the ideological impact of the fast capitalist story. Widespread acceptance of the inevitability of that story is a very powerful way of securing employee compliance with constant changes to, and intensification of, their work practices. Again there is nothing new in attempts to speed up work rates, and indeed these have been central to industrial disputes for centuries. The classic examples of struggles over attempts literally to speed up the moving assembly line of Fordist production are well documented in the labour process literature and elsewhere (e.g. Beynon, 1973; Edwards, 1979; Delbridge, 1998). Recent techniques associated with 'Toyota-ism' show precisely the same preoccupation with time as that found in Fordism: the much-documented Toyota–General Motors initiative at the NUMMI plant in California ensured that workers who had previously averaged 45 seconds work in the minute now work for 57 seconds (Basso, 2003: 64). Frederick Taylor's stopwatch has hardly been consigned to the pages of organization theory textbooks.

What is distinctive about the fast capitalist story, though, is precisely its ideological power. Instead of overt struggle over very visible speeding up, the idea of speed as necessary, obvious, incontestable and perhaps even desirable becomes insinuated into the very fabric of people's everyday lives and self-understandings. Indeed, it is noteworthy that some of the examples discussed by Hancock (2006) are clearly designed to *appeal* to, for example, graduate recruits. Speed can be seductive, so that rather than a manager standing over us, speeding up the assembly line, we ourselves have internalized speed as a taken-for-granted imperative (Hochschild, 1997). Clearly, this is an aspect of the more general accent on self-management described in Chapter 3.

the consequences of fast capitalism

These developments have a profound impact upon organizational practices and, therefore, upon work in ways that would have surprised our parents and grandparents. For much of the twentieth century the expectation was that the fruits of greater prosperity and mechanization would be a more leisured and reflective existence (Russell, 1935/2001), and this continued to be a cardinal assumption in, at least, western societies, right up to the 1970s. What has in fact happened is a much more frenetic and pressurized world for those in work. In the 1980s, an expression which defined the period was that 'greed is good'. Perhaps the expression that defines our own time is that 'speed is good'. A clear illustration of this can be found in the following example:

> The millionaire businessman Roy Aldridge ... boasts that his company Capita takes seven hours to make a decision reached in seven weeks by the civil service. (Chrisafis, 2003: 13)

But is speed really good? Although Capita is a hugely successful company with a turnover in 2006 of around £1,700 million (albeit no longer headed by Rod Aldridge, who resigned in 2006 following unproven allegations that government contracts were linked to his donations to the Labour Party), it has been involved in a series of controversies (Chrisafis, 2003). Capita is one of the companies of choice for the UK government for the privatization and/or sub-contracting of what had hitherto been state-provided services from driving tests to defence contracts to the leasing of ambulances. The long list includes individual learning accounts (which collapsed amidst fraud); criminal records (which failed to vet teachers in time to allow the school year to commence on time); and housing benefits and television licences (both systems encountering serious problems). For this reason, the firm is referred to by the satirical magazine *Private Eye* as 'Crapita'.

The case of individual learning accounts, to take just one of these examples, is revealing. Launched in 2000, the scheme cost £268 million until its collapse in 2002 due to widespread fraud on the part of bogus training providers. The National Audit Office (NAO) investigated what had happened and its head, Sir John Bourn, said:

> ... the *speed* with which the Department [for Education and Skills] implemented the scheme resulted in corners being cut ... which made fraudulent activities possible. (NAO 2002, *emphasis added*)

The potential dysfunctionality of fast capitalism is, indeed, one of the reasons why the private equity boom has attracted so much criticism. Whereas the speeding up of work and change is typically justified by the need for corporate survival, the criticism of private equity is that it simply sucks value out of a business, leaving it unfit to survive in the long term. The purpose of speeding up is not that of business efficiency as normally understood, but to allow complex financial engineering strategies, which generate potentially huge short-term rewards for investors as well as substantial fees for advisers. These strategies might include selling off premises or pension funds, or using them to leverage borrowing, so that trading the organization's assets becomes as significant, or more significant, than simply 'sweating' them for maximum productivity (see Folkman et al., 2006, for a detailed explanation).

Whether linked to the activities of private equity firms or not, there is no doubt that the contemporary workplace in the UK and elsewhere is characterized by an emphasis on speed. The UK has at various times been described as a manufacturing economy, a service economy, a post-industrial economy or a knowledge-intensive economy. Now, it has been suggested, it is an 'economy of permanent restructuring' (Froud et al., 2006). The implications of such an economy for organizations are profound. Drawing upon the work of Paul Virilio, mentioned earlier in this chapter, Roberts and Armitage (2006) explore the now notorious case of the US company Enron, which exemplifies the nature and the flaws of fast capitalist organizations. They depict Enron as having developed, since its foundation in

1985, from being a 'modern' organization, specializing in gas distribution, to a 'hypermodern' organization by the end of the twentieth century. As a hypermodern organization, its business became ever-more diversified and moved away from being based upon tangible assets, such as gas pipelines, to being a complex web of financial engineering and brand management. In this way, Enron may be said to exemplify Lash and Urry's (1994) insights into disorganized capitalism, in which physicality (actually producing 'things') gives way to an economy of symbolic manipulation. Enron was in a continuous and continual process of reorganization; work practices were constantly changing, staff turnover was massive. And this accent upon speed had its ironic counterpart in the rapidity of its demise for, as Roberts and Armitage point out, having become 'hypermodern' by the late 1990s, Enron collapsed in 2001.

This again may suggest the dysfunctionality of fast capitalism but, if so, there is little sign of let up. The respected business journalist Simon Caulkin (2007) discusses developments at ICI, one of the world's leading pharmaceutical companies. He points out that its global dominance was built on investment in long-term – meaning decades – of research and development work. Yet now, under the impact of pressure to conform to the business model of fast capitalism, ICI has transformed itself into a company concerned with dealmaking – mergers, de-mergers, acquisitions, divestments – and the whole panoply of what Caulkin calls '... the approved nostrums of financial management ... the institutionalised bad management of the kind that ticks all the boxes of the narrow playmakers by whose rules the UK's corporate economy now runs' (Caulkin, 2007). In other words, rather than being an organization to allow the gradual, long-term building of real products, Caulkin sees ICI as becoming a shell for the rapid, short-term generation of shareholder value and predicts that this mission will be the 'epitaph' of what was once a world-beating company.

But we do not have to rely upon predictions to see the problematic nature of fast capitalism. Consider the case of Northern Rock, the British bank. Formerly a locally based mutual building society following the conventional and cautious path of taking deposits from savers and lending to borrowers for house purchase, in 1997 it demutualized and subsequently embarked upon an altogether more ebullient business model in which money was raised through short-term borrowing on international financial markets and lending was made to people with poor credit histories in a way largely unrelated to their incomes or to the value of the houses they were buying. For a while all went well, Northern Rock grew rapidly and was fêted by financiers.[5] But in August 2007 a combination of fears about poor credit risks and a dry up of short-term lending funds destroyed the business model. The bank had to be bailed out by the Bank of England, became virtually worthless and, when no private buyer could be found to take it on, was nationalized in February 2008.

At one level this is just a story about a failed bank. But at another level it is an archetype for the deficiencies of fast capitalism. Traditional ways of doing business are discarded, indeed sneered at, in favour of rapid but unsustainable change, and localism gives way to globalized, anonymous financial wizardry. Beyond that, the ten-year period of Northern Rock's success coincided with, and was a part of, what Elliott and Atkinson (2007) call the 'Fantasy Island' economics which developed in the UK during that period. That is, it is an economy built upon individual consumer spending, which in turn is built upon debt, which in turn is based upon rising house prices which are themselves financed through debt. In the 1970s a person wishing to buy a home in Britain would need to establish with a lender – typically a mutual building society rooted in a particular place – a track record of saving, which would then form a deposit on a house, with the rest of the money, perhaps 80 per cent of the purchase price, borrowed through a mortgage equivalent to perhaps three times the annual income of the applicant. Such a system had problems of its own in terms of excluding people from home ownership, but distinct advantages over what replaced it. By the 1990s, banks such as, but by no means limited to, Northern Rock were lending five or more times the annual income of the applicant, and far from requiring a deposit would lend as much as 125 per cent of the value of a house. Typically, the extra money over and above the house purchase process would be used to consolidate existing debts or to pay for home improvements such as new kitchens. Even leaving aside Northern Rock's reliance upon short-term borrowing in the money markets to fund its lending, such lending is inherently unstable, relying upon continued house price

---

5   Something conveniently forgotten by those who now speak knowingly of the unsustainability of the Northern Rock business model, but which is consistent with the uncritical lionization of whatever happens to be the current success story in the form of case studies etc., as noted in many places throughout this book.

rises, low interest rates and upon the capacity of individuals to finance their indebtedness as other former mutual building societies, such as Bradford and Bingley, here found, albeit with less drastic effects than in the case of Northern Rock. In more extreme form, a similar process was underway in the United States in the so-called sub-prime mort-gage market (or, more piquantly, 'Ninja' mortgages for those with 'no income, no job and no assets'), which in turn precipitated the financial crisis of 2007 that triggered Northern Rock's collapse.

We can thus tie together a series of inter-related issues (they are related in a circular way, and so could be described in any order, not just the one given here). Fast capitalism is predicated upon the imme-diate satisfaction of consumer desires. But how can these be satisfied with what we have bought if it is immediately rendered obsolete by a 'new, improved' version of the same product? So rather than wait until something is saved for, it is purchased on credit (in 2007, per-sonal debt in the UK for the first time exceeded the annual GDP of that country). This credit is both a cause and a consequence of the huge, and hugely complex, global financial system that provides it; a system that also feeds vast quantities of investment capital to those companies which are obedient to the mantra of constant change and flexibility, thus feeding an economy of permanent re-structuring. Part and parcel of that re-structuring is the production of an ever-changing and widening array of consumer goods and services which can only be sustained by customers earning more or incurring debt to buy them; but the same re-structuring also reduces the employment secu-rity and rewards upon which that indebtedness is based. At every point within this scenario, *organizations* are implicated – and thus when we study organizations we are obligated to consider them not just as affected by, but as central to, fast capitalism. Organizations are the fulcrum which construct – which require – ever more 'productive' employees and ever more rapacious, and indebted, consumers.

Whether or not these 'fantasy' economics will be sustainable in the long-run remains to be seen, but in any case there are serious social problems associated with its persistence, and recently there have been some signs of a backlash against the culture associated with fast capitalism. Examples of this backlash include the work of the economist Richard Layard, who has broken open the question of the relationship between economics and well-being. In his book *Happiness* (Layard, 2005) he shows that increases in economic prosperity in the post-Second World War era have not made people happier, and have even made them less happy. In a somewhat related way, the popular psychologist Oliver James has identified the phenomenon of 'affluenza' (James, 2007) – the way that increased prosperity in the West has led to increasing levels of anxiety, selfishness, unsatisfying consumption and mental illness. A related recent popular tract, *Enough* by John Naish (2008), proposes the need for western consumers to avoid the trap that 'more is better' and to recognize the diminishing utility of consumption. This isn't conceived of as a matter of 'giving up' things, but rather recognizing for effectively self-interested reasons that excessive consumption is a bane rather than a boon (the more so if in the process we incur debt).

A fourth, again related but more academic, text is that of the sociologist Barry Schwartz. In *The Paradox of Choice* (2004), Schwartz says that the huge array of choices we in the West have to face is overloading and leads to dissatisfaction and unhappiness. The very success of economic productivity means that every good and service we consume comes in a myriad of different forms, whether we are talking about toothpaste, credit cards or holiday destinations. Moreover, particularly under the impact of privatization, individuals have to make choices in more and more areas of life, many of which have very significant consequences if you make the wrong choice – private pension provision, utility supplies and healthcare would be examples. Thus we (whether affluent conspicuous consumers, impoverished bargain hunters or simply people who need to access essential services) are kept increasingly busy just to keep up with the choices we must make. These choices are not simple, either. Perhaps in a shop you might choose between brand X and brand Y at two different prices, but trying to choose between the, say, mobile phone providers offering a complex array of tariffs combined with a range of 'free' goods and introductory bonuses is much more challenging. Even more complex, and rather more important, is the array of choices facing consumers of private health insurance in the US.

In this regard, it is interesting to reflect upon the role of the various kinds of consumer bodies and regulatory agencies which are supposedly concerned with protecting us against corporate abuse. But all these bodies can offer is the idea of exercising choice through 'shopping around', for example for the cheapest electricity supplier. This consigns us to a perpetual round of incessant activity as consumers, when perhaps what would be more desirable would simply be to have access to electricity at a reasonable price. Such simple regulation of prices used to be commonplace but is now perceived as old-fashioned 'statism'. Instead, the ideologues of fast capitalism, many governments included, insist that choice is always desirable, and more choice is always more desirable. But Schwartz suggests that, beyond a certain point, it is burdensome and anxiety provoking, as well as time consuming.

The re-fashioning of public services around the 'choice agenda' is a good example of this. In the UK, this agenda has lead to patients (or, rather, consumers of health care services) being offered choices about which hospital will treat them. You might, extols an NHS leaflet, choose the hospital with a high success rate in the operation you have to have. You might prefer the hospital with the lowest rate of post-operative infection. You might prefer the nearest hospital. These are clearly important choices, and will often have to be made in already stressful circumstances. But perhaps choice isn't at all helpful here: wouldn't it be more to the point to provide in every locality a decent hospital? A similar argument could be made about choice of schools.

This isn't just about the consequences for the individual. It also, of course, impacts upon social relations. As Schwartz says, 'being socially connected takes time' (2004: 110), but the combined pressures of speeded-up work, consumption and choice do not allow time for such connections to be made. This insight seems consistent with the influential analysis of Putnam (2000). Looking at data on the United States, Putnam suggests that over the last 30 years North Americans have begun to spend less and less time with friends, that families decreasingly often eat together or share leisure activities. In ways which have clear parallels to the literature already discussed, he says that it is social bonds, rather than prosperity, that lead to well-being, and that the growing erosion of such bonds are a significant cause of ill health and unhappiness. It seems clear that this declining 'social capital' (as Putnam calls it) is linked to the drive for economic competitiveness and the intensification of work. For whilst I have spoken repeatedly of these issues in terms of 'the West', it does seem to be the case that they are particularly a feature of those countries which have adopted the neo-liberal model of work and welfare with which fast capitalism is most closely associated. Countries such as France, Italy, Spain and, especially, the Scandinavian countries seem to have been less affected.

What this suggests, then, is that the malaise under discussion is not simply the inevitable consequence of capitalist markets, or even of affluence, but is something to do with the way that life, and perhaps in particular work, is organized. It is certainly the case that work demands in the US and the UK are much higher than in the 'happier countries': in 2002, UK and US workers did an average of around 2,000 hours' work per year, whereas in Germany, France,

Italy, Denmark and the Netherlands the average was around 1,700 hours (Layard, 2005: 50). Being more busy seems to make people less happy and make societies less cohesive.

However, there is a distinction to be drawn between the issues of time and hard work and those of fast capitalism. After all, our grand-parents typically worked many more than 2,000 hours a year, yet arguably experienced more robust social bonds and higher degrees of 'social capital'. So it is not, simply, that working hard leaves less time for the cultivation of social relations. It is more to do with the consequences of 'an economy of permanent restructuring'. The con-sequences of such an economy are to make it 'rootless': unconnected with places or communities. Richard Sennett's (1998) research is very revealing on this point. Based upon studies of several individuals and groups of workers (including some whom he had studied 20 years previously), he argues that it is the radical disorganization of work associated with the 'new capitalism' which has disoriented and even destroyed what had previously been reasonably solid social relations. In particular, the erosion of stable career structures where the work ethic was rewarded and which existed within reasonably stable orga-nizations embedded within communities has been a major factor in eroding trust and well-being. Instead, short-term contracts, geograph-ical mobility and constant change characterize the workplace. As he puts it in a later work, 'a shortened framework of institutional time [i.e. speeding up] lies at the heart of this social degradation' (Sennett, 2006: 181). This is a much more political analysis than that supplied by Putnam, for example, and in a sense brings us back full circle to Marx and Engels: the societal consequences of an economic system in which 'all that is solid melts into air.'

the end of management

Fast capitalism inevitably creates winners and losers. The winners, at least financially, are not just the owners of corporations but also the investment bankers, management consultants and financial engi-neers who broker the deals that keep the merry-go-round spinning. Some might say that consumers also benefit in terms of an ever-greater array of goods and services at cheaper prices. I would doubt this, for the reasons given earlier about the dubious benefits of greater affluence and choice. Consumption is rather like heroin: it gives you a high at first but in the end it offers diminishing returns and, like any other addiction (cigarettes in my case), only gives pleasure to the extent that it feeds your addiction: if the addiction didn't exist, nor would the pleasure.

A more sophisticated variant of the idea that there is a broad range of winners from fast capitalism argues that many individuals reap its rewards through their pension schemes, which are major investors in the financial markets. This is an important issue in terms of the way that organizations, employees, consumers and the political and economic system are linked together (see Minns, 2001, for detailed analysis). Nevertheless, it has considerable limitations. First, any benefit which the ordinary pensioner receives from involvement in the financial markets is very small beer when compared with the rewards reaped by financiers. When a tiny number of people are gorging on an enormous loaf, it seems scant justification that a larger number of people (but still by no means everyone) have access to the crumbs. And, in any case, even in the bull markets of the early to mid-2000s, pension schemes, especially of the more generous final salary sort, were increasingly pronounced unsustainable and many have been closed. There is therefore pressure to reduce even this minor sharing of the rewards, and this seems set to increase precisely because of the demands within fast capitalism to cut such 'wasteful' overheads. Indeed, pensions are part of the apparatus of security that, according to Boltanski and Chiapello (2007), formed part of the 'second spirit of capitalism' which is now being displaced by current developments. Second, exposure to the risks of the financial markets is by no means an unalloyed virtue. On the contrary, it potentially makes pensioners very vulnerable, as, most notoriously, policyholders with Equitable Life discovered when it turned out that they would not receive the benefits they had been promised, and had paid for. Pensioners in company schemes are also vulnerable to the wind-up of such schemes if the company goes bankrupt or defaults on its obligations. But finally, and from my point of view perhaps most importantly, the proposition that one should welcome the intensification of work because it possibly leads to deferred rewards in the form of future pension rights contributes to locking the door on a highly self-disciplinary prison. Indeed, it seems to me that those who trumpet pensions as a defence of the casino capitalism from which they benefit (or with which they identify) are aiming at exactly this.

In any case, consumption and pensions aside, the biggest losers of fast capitalism are, as they have always been, the poorest and most vulnerable people in the Developing World whose traditional communities are most dramatically displaced and who are most readily corralled into sweatshop labour. And it is not just here where people are organized in degrading ways. For example, it was not in the Developing World but in California, one of the richest places in the world, where factory workers were forbidden to use the toilet but instead told to urinate in their clothes, so that no production time was lost (Perelman, 2005: 66–7). In a less vicious but functionally related way, the losers are those in the West exposed to ever-increasing work-loads and the declining permanency of employment. It is easy to make a critique of fast capitalism by reference to its obvious abuses, but to do so invites the relatively affluent to see the problem in these terms, rather than recognizing that they, themselves, suffer albeit in the more subtle and complex ways I indicated in the previous section. There are also wider things which are lost, as I have suggested, in terms of social bonds and community stability. But one particular casualty of fast capitalism is management.

As I argued in Chapter 2, the high status of management was constructed over a long historical period as something necessary and valuable, to the point were it could be described by Peter Drucker in the mid-1950s as a bulwark of western civilization. Fifty years on, that looks an almost absurd proposition. Instead, even managerially inclined writers can claim that 'There is a strong case that management ... could finally die out early in the twenty-first century' (Koch and Godden, 1996: 1).

One aspect of the decline of management is the way that the employment prospects and working conditions of, especially, middle managers have eroded. I have already suggested in Chapters 3 and 4 that this is so as a consequence of the increasing accent upon self-management. There is ample evidence that middle management has been under attack, illustrated by the demotic utterances of the 'guru' Tom Peters: 'Middle management ... is dead ... It's over, d'ya hear? Over. Over. Over' (cited in Thomas and Dunkerley, 1999).

I think we can interpret this to mean that Tom Peters thinks that middle management is over. It is tempting to dismiss such hyperbole, and it bears saying that claims about the imminent demise of management have been made for a very long time (e.g. Fletcher, 1973), but there is now a mass of well-researched studies attesting to the same thing (e.g. Wheatley, 1992; Heckscher, 1995; Thomas and Dunkerley, 1999; Kodz et al., 2003). Taken together, we can at the very least say that the shine has gone off management as compared to its heyday in the post-war era.

This is illuminated by a study that some colleagues and I conducted (Brocklehurst et al., 2007). It was initially concerned with the knowledge brought by senior managers into the classroom when undertaking an Executive MBA programme. In the course of conducting interviews with these managers, we noticed that *not one* used the term 'manager' to describe themselves. So we conducted a follow-up study with a smaller number of them, drawn from different kinds of organizations and sectors, and asked about this. They told us that they did indeed abjure the term 'manager' for two broad reasons. First, they saw it as an over-used term in that it no longer denoted a person of any great seniority but was routinely used for quite low-level supervisory jobs. This is not quite to posit the 'end of management', but rather to say that it has spread to the point where it becomes meaningless. Second, and more importantly, they saw 'manager' as having a pejorative meaning of someone who was inflexible, unproductive and – horror of horrors – bureaucratic.

Clearly this links with the widespread demonization of bureaucracy discussed in Chapter 4, and by the same token the terms which these 'managers' preferred to use to describe themselves were part of the new lexicon of organizations. These terms included 'leader', 'entrepreneur', 'change agent' and 'consultant'. Of course Executive MBA students are a very particular group of managers, but this makes my point in that what their particularity consists of is that they are ambitious high-flyers who have a degree of choice as to how to describe themselves: and they choose not to describe themselves as managers. Moreover, what they were saying is consistent with the dominant image of the 'fast manager' identified in more theoretical writings (Thrift, 2005: 130–52). This poses particular issues for management education, which are discussed in Chapter 6.

The significance of this can be linked back to the three broad explanation of the *rise* of management that I reviewed in Chapter 2. To reprise, these were that management arose because of its technical advantages of co-ordination; because it delivered control of workers; and as a result of the manoeuvrings of an elite group. What can now be suggested is that all of these reasons for management have eroded. The increasing tendency to subcontract and to buy in expertise on a temporary basis suggests a shift from hierarchical to market-based co-ordination; the increasing accent on self-management obviates the need to external management of labour. But perhaps most important – given that, as we have seen, the extent of these new organizational practices is debatable – is the way that management has failed to perpetuate its elite status.

At the heart of that failure, I think, are the issues of fast capitalism raised in this chapter. The original managerial revolution thesis propounded most famously by James Burnham (1945) was, in summary, that:

> … the largest corporations are now more often than not controlled by managers not owners … managerial incentive systems are more closely tied to criteria other than company profitability … [and] as a result … most large firms are now oriented towards objectives beyond strict profit-maximization. (Useem, 1984: 29)

This, allied to the development of a technocratic welfare and military state during the Cold War period, accounts for Drucker's belief in the pivotal place of management in Western civilization. But as Sennett (2006) explains, this model of 'social capitalism' has come apart not least as a result of the way that investors now have far more power in relation to the managers of corporations than they did in the mid-twentieth century. As financial markets were deregulated, massive flows of capital began to search out investment opportunities:

> Initially managers thought they were dealing with investors familiar to them from the past, that is, largely passive institutions and individuals. The workings of a firm would be confirmed at annual meetings where the only challenges would come from oddly dressed elderly ladies or vegetarian activists. The managers were soon disabused. Investors became active judges; a turning point … occurred when pension funds, controlling fast quantities of capital, began actively pressuring management. The increasing sophistication of financial instruments like the leveraged buyout meant that investors could make or break corporations while its management stood helplessly by. (Sennett, 2006: 39)

Under these conditions, managers gave way to financiers who became, in the novelist Tom Wolfe's now famous, or infamous, phrase, the self-styled 'masters of the universe'. It was and is not enough for the management of a company to turn a profit: they are constantly pressurized to increase that profit under threat of a new management team being brought in. Moreover, the time-frame within which profits and profit increases were required became shorter and shorter, and the speed with which trading could occur became faster and faster. In short, the capacity of management to pursue interests that diverged from profit-maximization has become significantly reduced, and with it the basis upon which it could be sustained as an elite. This argument should be finessed a little, though. Froud et al. (2006) argue convincingly, and in detail, that the financialization of business around shareholder value actually benefited managers more than shareholders, as the former gained substantial pay increases. However, these were, and are, the senior managers of large global corporations. The flip-side is the much larger white-collar 'underclass' whose travails in the US are documented by Ehrenreich (2006). These are the laid-off middle managers consigned to increasing poverty and despair by the disjuncture between their former wealth, status and security and their redundancy to fast capitalism. So whilst it would be excessive to claim that management has died out, certainly it is looking more than a little sickly.

There is, however, an apparent paradox in this. For, despite the travails of management in fast capitalism, there has been no corresponding demise in *managerialism*. That is to say, the insinuation of a managerial, instrumentally rational, way of apprehending the world at large, work organizations included, continues unabated. Within organizations, we see a proliferation of attempts to measure and manage performance and the relentless attention to strategies, values, mission, quality, re-organization and so on discussed in previous chapters. Outside the organization, as Hancock and Tyler (2008) show, more and more of everyday life is seen as being amenable to management. It now, perhaps, becomes clearer why in Chapter 2 I was at such pains to distinguish between management and managers. For whilst management in the sense of managers may be coming to an end, management in the sense of a managerial way of looking at the world is in robust and swaggering form. Indeed, it is an irony that even as the flaws of the fast capitalist model become apparent, the idea that it should be adopted within the public sector grows ever stronger as the financial engineers, having exhausted the gains from destroying the social capitalist settlement of the post-war era, greedily eye the profits they could make from the state sector, which is the last vestige of that settlement.

conclusion

Fast capitalism does not represent a new epoch, and claims that it does are dangerous because they easily slide into the idea that it is something inevitable, a matter of the inexorable sweep of history rather than a determinate matter of the social and political choices we have made and are making. Rather, it is consistent with what relatively unregulated capitalism has always been. Indeed, what is beginning to be clear is that the period of social capitalism – that is, a regulated capitalism linked to welfarism – was particular to the four or five decades after the great depression and the Second World War. Nor are speculative booms new. By the same token, the current situation is not itself likely to be enduring. Much of fast capitalism, both in the frenzy of merger and acquisition and private equity activity and the consumption boom, is fuelled by credit. It is highly unlikely that this will be sustainable and is itself particular to circumstances of cheap money, much of it derived from the wash of investment funds generated by, in particular, Chinese economic growth in the early years of this century. Alternatives to fast capitalism are not just easy to envisage, but are likely to emerge precisely because the circumstances which have given rise to it will change – perhaps they are doing so even as I write.

Nevertheless, the consequences of fast capitalism for organizations are real and, in my view, deleterious. The economy of signs and space identified by Lash and Urry (1994) entails what is called 'deracination' – in other words, the destruction of roots. When there is little connection between places and communities on the one hand and production and consumption on the other, then the result is a certain kind of suffering (Bourdieu, 1999). Organization theory has by and large been so preoccupied with slavishly and unquestioningly following the idea of an inevitable new epoch that it has had almost nothing to say about this.

Outside of organization theory, though, there are people, ideas and movements which are trying to interrogate, and find alternatives to, fast capitalism. The 'slow movement', as its name implies, is explicitly concerned with challenging, negating and replacing what they would call the cult of speed. The origins of this as a 'movement' (although no doubt the ideas it draws upon are older) lie in the development of the notion of 'slow food' as an antidote to the growth of fast food (Petrini, 2001; Kummer, 2002). Whereas fast food is about no more than 're-fuelling' in between activities, slow food is about taking time to savour and enjoy not just the experience of eating but also that of preparing food and of sharing it with other people.

What began as a slow food movement has become a wider set of proposals for alternative ways of living, which all share the desire to resist the continual attempt by others to make us do things faster and our own internalized desire to do so. Although as a movement it is fragmented and still emergent, many of its tenets have been articulated by Carl Honoré (2004). Honoré writes, for example, of slow cities where striding is replaced by strolling; of slow medicine where a quick consultation and drug prescription is replaced by unhurried and holistic healing; of slow parenting where pushing children into a hectic range of high-achieving activities is replaced by more leisured play and emotional connection; and of course slow work.

The slow movement may seem marginal and idealistic (and, perhaps, predicated upon choices which are most available to the already affluent), but it does at least open up the possibility of a different vision of life to that offered by fast capitalism. One of the things which history teaches us is that ideas which appear ludicrous at one time appear common-sensical in others – that slavery is wrong; that the sexes have equal political rights, for example. The slow movement offers a glimpse of a desirable life, which fast capitalism largely fails to do. It is clearly related to more diffuse calls for localism. These again derive initially from thinking about food as something which should be related to locality rather than the year-round availability of each and every foodstuff. This in turn connects to one of the major sources of alternative thinking, the environmental movement. This would suggest that fast capitalism is simply unsustainable in terms of natural resources and the climate. Perhaps in the past such views would have seemed both freakish and puritanical. But the freakishness has become increasingly mainstream as the evidence of climate change accumulates, whilst the Puritanism is undermined by the increasing evidence that affluence and consumption are, beyond a certain point, unsatisfying and perhaps even dissatisfying.

The implications of slowness and localism for organizations are very profound. They would put work back to a human scale of time and place. They are not arguments for the abolition of capitalism, still less for the replacement of capitalism with state control. We do not need to feel stuck within such hidebound oppositions. Roberts and Armitage's (2006) analysis of the Enron scandal, Caulkin's (2007) fears about ICI and Froud et al.'s (2006) studies of financial engineering and private equity, as well as many similar analyses, pose very sharp questions about the sustainability of 'fast capitalism'. Ultimately, organizations need to deliver something beneficial in terms of real goods and services, to do so reliably and durably, and to meet the needs of people – both employees and customers – above and beyond shareholders.

At the time of writing there is a global financial crisis or 'credit crunch', which I alluded to earlier when I discussed the case of Northern Rock, caused by a complex pyramid of debt. Individuals have borrowed more than they can afford in order to consume at the levels deemed normal. Their debts have been packaged up and traded between financial institutions, which now doubt whether the loans can be called in. These institutions are now wary of lending, and in any case have less money to lend, and so have reduced credit to the private equity firms which rely on borrowing to fuel company takeovers as well as to individual borrowers. Although the financial institutions decry state intervention, they are being bailed out by governments and central banks who fear a collapse of confidence in the financial system, the recent de facto nationalization of the huge US mortgage institutions Freddie Mac and Fannie Mae being a prime example. There is nothing new in that, for again and again free market ideologues who abjure regulation rely upon it when times get hard (Perelman, 2005) so that although the profit of private enterprise is indeed private – that is, enjoyed by the few – the risk is socialized – that is, shared by all of us.[6]

It may then be that the credit crunch is giving the empirical lie to the great myth which underpins fast capitalism: the myth of a 'new economy' based not upon the production of goods and services but upon some mystical 'value'. I am certain that this is a myth, and the failure to recognize this is the real flaw in the thinking of those who would proclaim a new epoch. The notion that we inhabit a 'weightless economy' (e.g. Leadbetter, 1999), or similar formulations, cannot survive encounters with the heavy rock of reality, as happened for example when Russia closed off energy supplies to the Ukraine; when Hurricane Katrina caused an almost complete societal breakdown in the US; or when fuel protestors came within a day or two of bringing the UK to a standstill. These are very different cases, but what they have in common is that they point to the enduring truth that organizations are about something concrete, and that the 'economy of signs and space' identified by social theorists and celebrated by the ideologues of fast capitalism is simply and unequivocally unsustainable.

---

6   The Northern Rock case is again instructive: at the time of writing, following nationalization, the shareholders are seeking to be generously recompensed despite the fact that the bank has failed and in defiance, be it noted, of the standard argument used to justify shareholders receiving rewards, i.e. that they *risk* losing everything. Apparently this argument no longer holds when that risk transpires!

What, then, of managers? At a general level one might say that the demise of a self-interested managerial elite, like the demise of Communist *apparatchiks* or Catholic ecclesiastics, is just their bad luck. Yet it is perturbing that highly competent managers who used to keep companies and public infrastructure going have been swept aside by fast capitalism. It seems to me that in almost any conceivable future society those kinds of dedicated, competent managers will be needed, and that they had a dignity and purpose akin to the rooted communities of manual workers which have now been displaced.

The most important issue is to re-pose the question of what the purpose of human collective – i.e. organizational – activity is and whether current social and economic arrangements deliver it. This would be to open up the fundamental question of social philosophy: what is the good life and how is it to be achieved? We should not seek to answer this question in terms of a return to some previous golden age. Not only is such time-travel impossible, it would also be undesirable: any supposed golden age inevitably, on closer examination, proves flawed. Nor need we answer this question in binary terms of capitalism or communism, and indeed few would now do so. It is quite possible to envisage systems that retain private property and market exchange but which are based upon local economies and work practices which are supportive of, rather than damaging to, human potentials and the environment. Despite the contemporary stress upon shareholder value and free markets as unquestionably desirable, the historical truth is that capitalism has been at its most successful when regulated towards the consideration of wider concerns about social well-being. If fast capitalism is indeed as deleterious to that well-being – both in terms of production and consumption – as has been suggested in this chapter, then that begins to make out the need for alternatives.

One of my favourite writers is the philosopher and theologian Simone Weil. She had much of interest to say about work and organizations, as I have noted elsewhere (Grey, 1996). Amongst her works is a book called *The Need for Roots* (Weil, 1949). It is a difficult and complex book, as much spiritual as social scientific, but informed by her own time as a factory worker. She says that we need order, responsibility, hierarchy and honour if we are to live well. She did not mean the 'order' of the call centre script; not the 'responsibility' of the empowered employee; not the 'hierarchy' of the petty bureaucrat; not the 'honour' of the Masonic lodge. Rather, Weil expounds the dignity which comes from settled, meaningful work within settled, comprehensible communities. It is precisely the opposite of the endless deracination proposed by fast capitalism. There are better ways to organize than one which requires more and more work to buy more and more things when neither the work nor the things make us happy. The apologists for fast capitalism insist that that which opposes them is some kind of old-fashioned elitism, but my objection to their world view is emancipatory rather than onservative: they are wedded to the inevitability of the future, no matter what the consequences, whereas I think we have choices. That we have not, thus far, exercised those choices as wisely as we might need not mean that we are debarred from doing so in the future. We should not separate the study of organizations from these choices and yet all too often we do. In the next chapter I will explain why this is so.

6

Business Schools and the Myth of Management Education

Processing plants for the faking of intellectual authority.
Thomas Frank

I have referred at several times in this book to a salient fact. Almost all of the study of organizations (whether this means research study or the following of courses) takes place in university business and management schools. This was not always the case, since many classic studies of organizations were conducted in sociology, psychology, economics or other departments and disciplines, but now it is overwhelmingly true. This, I suggest, means that the study of organizations is itself organized; that is, it can only be understood in terms of the particular institutional arrangements and purposes of business and management schools. I have suggested several times that the understanding of organizations I want to urge differs from 'the mainstream', and this means, primarily, the business school mainstream. Initially this may seem a matter of small importance. What can it possibly matter where a subject is taught? We wouldn't expect physics to be different if it were taught in a Department of Physics or a School of Science. But the study of organizations is different, precisely because – despite the claims of positivists – its subject matter is not value-free but value-laden. So when it gets studied in business schools it gets studied in particular ways. The purpose of this chapter is to explore the context in which organizations are studied and to explain why it matters.

Almost all business schools claim, and most – although by no means all – of their students expect, that management education produces better managers (this claim is perhaps made more at MBA than undergraduate level). Like studying law or medicine, management education supposedly contributes to the ideal of producing the professional manager. Admittedly, it has never been the case that, unlike doctors and lawyers, you are required to take a management degree to practice as a manager, but the implicit and usually explicit promise made to people who study at business schools is that they will acquire a knowledge that equips them for practice. If you are such a person I would guess that you already entertain some doubts as to whether this expectation will be realized – doubts presumably compounded if you have been recommended this book by your lecturer. Sadly, perhaps, your doubts are fully justified. For there is *absolutely no evidence* that taking a management course has any effect at all upon making people better managers, and it is even possible that it makes people worse managers. Business schools are for the most part founded on a myth which distorts organization theory. But, paradoxically, recognizing the myth actually enables managers and others to gain something from the study of organizations.

This may seem like bad news, given that students have typically paid quite a bit of money and/or foregone earnings because the courses they take have been marketed with the claim that they will enhance managerial performance. The good news might be that although studying management doesn't make better managers, it does often make more employable and higher-paid managers, so all is not lost. But comforting or not, this is a very odd state of affairs. People who study medicine or engineering or law or science expect, and are probably not wrong to expect, to be better doctors, engineers, lawyers or scientists than they otherwise would be. Similarly, if I am ill, or want to build a bridge, make a will or know about physical laws, then I will have more confidence in a trained rather than an untrained doctor, engineer, lawyer or scientist. Yet I hardly care – and I am certain I am not unique – whether my manager has studied management or not.

This doesn't necessarily mean that management education is useless, but it does mean that its use is different to what is typically claimed for and expected of it. It also means that there is something about management education which needs to be better understood. For there is no doubt that management education is important. In the UK (in 2005/06, the latest year for which figures are available), about one in seven undergraduates study management or business, making it the single largest subject, and many more students take a management or business option as part of their degree, whilst some 27,000 students are registered for an MBA and another 23,000 take other postgraduate degrees in management (Association of Business Schools, 2008). The UK produces more MBAs than the whole of the rest of Europe put together, and the US produces some ten times more than the UK. The MBA is becoming, in Europe, and has become, in the US, the key to entry to the upper echelons of business and, increasingly, the public sector. In Europe and the US, as well as Australia, New Zealand, India, China and many other countries, the numbers of management students and management degree programmes continues to rise. In the UK, prospective cabinet ministers of the embryonic Labour government prior to its election in 1997 were sent to a management school to learn how to manage their ministries. In the US, for the first time in history, the President (George W. Bush) holds an MBA, from Harvard. With all this demand, they must be doing something right.

Well – no, actually. Not if the deal is about making better managers. It has given me, and I hope will continue to give me, reasonably lucrative employment, so perhaps I shouldn't complain (I'll come back to this later). But management education is deeply flawed, and will continue to be so until some fairly fundamental truths are recognized. I suppose that central to these – and how arrogant this sounds, but of course I believe in my arguments or else why would I make them? – is what I have been trying to emphasize in this book. Namely, that the conceit of management knowledge to offer a way of exerting systematic, predictable control over organizations is just that, a conceit: flawed, incoherent in theory, unrealizable in practice.[1]

At the heart of this are the issues of unintended consequences, agency and resistance discussed throughout this book. And I want now to make a very fundamental point about these issues. Most critiques of management flow from some version of a political position (either left-wing defences of working-class rights or right-wing

---

1   Some readers of the first edition of this book made the point that some business schools, especially those with a strong research base, do in fact teach something close to what I am advocating in this book. This may be so, and I acknowledged in the Introduction that it is becoming a more common approach. But – and it is a big but – where this occurs it almost never forms the explicit claim made about courses in marketing literature to prospective students. I know of some, but very, very few business schools which admit that their courses have no impact upon managerial performance. Moreover, even where a different approach is adopted, it is typically done on particular modules inside an overall programme that takes the mainstream perspective. I will concede that I am generalizing in this chapter but I do not concede my claim that the mainstream is what dominates. Indeed, how else could it be the mainstream?

defences of individual liberty) which rejects the case for managerial control (to put it at its most generic). I share, rather eclectically, elements of both these political positions. But that is not the point. The point is not simply whether or not management should exert control of others, it is whether it *can*. My assertion in this book is that it cannot; and in terms of this chapter, this means that I assert that the pretensions of management education to teach techniques for effective management are unfounded. Note that my claim here is quite different from those (of whom there have over the years been many) who argue that management education is in need of reform so as to make it more helpful to managerial effectiveness. I am arguing that any such reform would be doomed to failure, because its aim is unrealizable *in principle*.

what's the problem?

Apart from the arguments I have been making throughout this book, consider this: if it were possible in principle to create a managerially effective form of management education, why has it not yet happened? It is not as if management schools are a new phenomenon. They started in the 1880s, when the first such school, Wharton, opened in Pennsylvania, endowed by Joseph Wharton who, by a pleasing coincidence – which I mentioned in Chapter 1 – was the owner of the Bethlehem Steel Works where Frederick Taylor had conducted his work on scientific management.

Or is it such a coincidence? The context for the development of management education was very much that of the emergence of complex, large-scale industry and, associated with that, the growing separation of ownership and control. This led to a growing need for professional managers, which in turn fed the development of management education. On this account, there should indeed be a link between managerial effectiveness and management education. But, of course, things are not that simple. To take just one aspect of this complexity: if management education is an inevitable function of the need for managers in large-scale industry, then why was (and is) it so much more prevalent in North America than in Germany, France, Japan and (at least until recently) the UK, even though some of these economies industrialized as early, or earlier, and as extensively, as the US? But all that said, the Wharton 'coincidence' is an interesting one because it should alert us to the fact that, just as management bears the imprint of nineteenth-century North American industry, so too does much management education (Engwall and Zamagni, 1998).

This has had important consequences for the shape and development of management education, and continues to do so. One issue is that, as I mentioned at the beginning of this chapter, a great deal of formal management education takes place within universities. There was a long (and not yet dead) tradition of such education being conducted in commercial training institutions from the outset of the industrial revolution (see Pollard, 1965) and, especially outside the US, that tradition persisted for a long time with neither assistance nor threat from the university sector. By the time university management education got going in a big way elsewhere this meant that the US model was dominant, since it was just about the only model going, and this led, in particular, to the MBA becoming the flagship postgraduate management qualification.

This was not just for want of a better model, however. It is also intimately bound up with the 'American management mystique' (Locke, 1996) to which I alluded in Chapter 3. If American management was superior to that of other countries, and if this was supported by the American management education system, then ergo American management education must be superior. The fact that each link in this argument is, at the very best, debatable didn't stop it being influential. In any case, there was power politics at play. Much of the development of, at least, European management education was bound up with the Cold War in the period following the end of the Second World War. American foreign policy at the time was concerned that continuing instability and economic crisis in Western Europe would render it vulnerable to Communism. Such a view informed the reconstruction of Europe under the Marshall Plan.

On a much smaller scale, it contributed to the growth of business schools, often underpinned by American finance and employing US trained faculty – INSEAD in France being a prime example. In the UK, it was not until the 1960s that significant developments in management education began with the establishment of graduate business schools at London (LBS) and Manchester (MBS), and this development was less linked to the politics of post-war reconstruction and more to ongoing concerns within the UK about falling relative productivity levels. Yet, again, and especially in the case of LBS, the model was North American.

It continues to be the case that management education is dominated by a US model – the curriculum, the textbooks, the case studies are typically derived from North America. That is not to deny a good deal of variation, especially within Europe, but, particularly for those schools aspiring to elite international status, the US model still dominates, at least so far as MBA courses are concerned. Undergraduate provision is more varied, again perhaps especially in Europe, partly because it tends to draw on indigenous social science traditions. However, as anyone who has studied on any management course will know, a great deal of the subject matter and research base is from the US.[2]

That last observation points to the fact that, although I have been talking so far about management education, there are very important and obvious links between management education and the knowledge generated by management research. Much of what is taught on management courses is the product of management research; most university management educators are also researchers and vice versa. From this point of view, too, management education bears an American imprint not least because, in simple quantitative terms, management research has been going for longer and in a greater volume there than anywhere else in the world.

So take any textbook on organizations and consider a topic which appears in just about all of them: motivation. Maslow, Herzberg, Vroom, Lawler and Adams will all feature, but you will be hard pressed to find much work done outside the US. Does this matter? I'm certainly not denying that there is plenty of good and interesting research done in North America. I'm not 'anti-American', to use a phrase with unfortunate antecedents and much contemporary currency. But the US dominance of organization theory does mean that a great deal of it reflects particular intellectual traditions and, especially in more recent decades, some particular features which I will come to in a moment. Additionally, it is not just the researchers but the people on whom research is conducted that matters here. The organizational theorist Roy Jacques (1996), in one of the best studies of management thought I have read, makes the telling observation

2   Some readers of the first edition have also made the point that 'Europe is different', and to some extent I agree. But we should not get carried away with this. At both the 'top' and 'bottom' ends – in terms of prestige – the US model holds sway, even where the schools in question lie outside the US geographically. It might be better to say that the exceptions are in some 'middle ranking' business schools in, I would guess, the UK, Scandinavia and one or two other places.

that what is known about organizations in terms of its classic research base is largely what is known about white, North American, male manual workers and students in the 1950s and 1960s.

Perhaps it will seem as if I have moved away from the issue of whether management education makes people better managers, towards some more general complaints about management research in general and North American management research in particular. But these issues are all bound up together. At the very least, if the knowledge base of management education is primarily North American, does this not suggest that there are some limitations on the extent to which it can be generalized to other cultures and continents?

Moreover, I should clarify that what I am saying here is not really something about the US but about the dominant orthodoxy. This orthodoxy overlaps to some large extent with US research, just because of the historical dominance which I have pointed to. This now means that the 'best' research journals are by definition mainly North American and the work they carry has to conform to certain norms. This, with an inevitable circularity, becomes the 'best' research and is reproduced in the textbooks. Now all this might well be true in many other fields, especially sciences, but there it does no great harm because there is quite a degree of international consensus about what constitutes good science. In research on management and organizations that is not so.

Ironically, during the period that American management education was being exported to other countries, within the US itself it was the subject of some concern. Specifically, as a series of reports (for example, Ford Foundation, Carnegie) in the 1950s highlighted, the concern was that what was being taught had little scientific status, academic rigour and a poor research base. What was needed was to produce a reliable body of scientifically-tested knowledge which could then be taught to managers who would have the basis on which to decide and act in ways that would have predictable results. This view, which I described as positivism in the Introduction to this book, derived from a particular, and at the time quite widely held, belief about the nature of social science in general. It was enthusiastically taken up within US business schools where, increasingly (for this had by no means been true before), organizational and management research was done.

Today, much of the consensus that social science can be thought of that way has evaporated. But this has had very little impact upon what are now the institutionalized norms of US business schools and the research journals they run – norms which, because of the position of the US in management education and its wider economic, political and military dominance, are highly influential around the world. Thus research in the US continues to be dominated by large-scale quantitative studies, hypothesis testing and the search for causal relationships between variables. In other words, the dream of positivist science remains firmly in place, to define what 'good' research is and to form the bulk of textbook knowledge.

But now we come full circle. For what is striking is the observation with which I began this chapter. For all that we have had, say, in five decades of research in this mould, there is still almost nothing in the way of predictive laws and established causal relations that can be found in organizations. Therefore there is no body of knowledge which, when mastered by students, can be used as a reliable basis for action by managers. Instead, there are reams of abstract statistics which tell us – well, nothing at all. There are all kinds of theoretical and philosophical ways we can explain this – I've touched on them lightly throughout this book – but in some ways one hardly needs to grasp these to take on board a brutally pragmatic truth. The positivist way has not worked.

So why does it persist? At one level it is because those involved have got a huge amount invested in it – not just financially, though that too is true, but psychologically. But, at another level, it persists because it is a convenient fiction for all concerned which allows management education to get on with what it is really about. For if what I have said is true, then how can the enduring success of management education be explained when it apparently fails to 'do what it says on the tin'? In the next section I will try to explain it.

so what's going on?

Consider this:

> In Honduras, when filling out a particularly large order on a tight deadline, factory managers have been reported injecting workers with amphetamines to keep them going on forty-eight-hour marathons. (Klein, 2000: 216)

This story might be regarded as a one-off anomaly of no particular interest, were it not for the fact that it fits a pattern of abuse for which Klein, and many others, have provided considerable evidence. For example, the International Labour Organization has identified the existence of some 850 'export processing zones' in which some 27 million people work (cited in Klein, 2000: 215). It is in these zones that the bulk of the world's 'sweatshops' are to be found and, whilst the amphetamine example would be at the extreme end of the spectrum, working conditions are notoriously poor. For example, in the Nike factory in China during the 1990s, workers were paid 16 cents an hour for a 77–84 hour week (1998 figures). Overtime was not paid extra, there were fines for refusing to work overtime and corporal punishment was used (Klein, 2000: 474, where 16 similar examples are listed). Such practices are not illegal within export processing zones, and they are mandated by the growth of international free trade agreements underpinned by institutions such as the World Trade Organization. The politics of these issues are of course fraught and, at the present time, in flux. But for present purposes, it is enough to say there is well-documented evidence for the existence of these kinds of organizational experiences as a reality for many of the world's employees.

Yet these experiences rarely figure in management textbooks used in business schools where a more sanitized, if not sentimentalized, version of the organization is to be found. Peter Senge, for example, approvingly quotes a CEO who tells us that:

> The total development of our people is essential to achieving our goal of corporate excellence … the fullest development of people is on an equal plane with financial success … practicing the virtues of life and business success are not only compatible but enrich one another. (Senge, 1993: 143–4)

The tone here is rather gushing, but it is clearly consistent with the messages found in many corporate mission statements ('our people are our greatest asset') and, in various ways, in the nostrums of textbooks on organizations and human resource management. Very few other subjects within the management curriculum give any consideration at all to working conditions, except through the desiccated language of 'variable costs' and similar euphemisms. How are we to square this with the realities of, at least, a significant part of the world economy? Why, if such practices are, apparently, necessary to corporate competitiveness, do business schools not openly teach them? Surely they would if management education was really about producing more effective professional managers. But I have already claimed they are about something else.

management education and socialization

What could this 'something else' be? The most extreme way of understanding management education would be to see it as an entirely cynical charade. Thus, so long as no one knew, management students could spend their courses, say, sitting in a dark room and it would not matter since the value of management education is purely symbolic and credentialist – just a matter of putting letters after people's names. This, of course, would be difficult to sustain both because it would always be likely to be found out and also because the negative identity it would offer participants and providers would be almost unbearable. Yet a less extreme version of this does, it has been argued, pervade management education. Watson (1996) refers to a 'contract of cynicism' in management education wherein students accept, and faculty delivers, knowledge which both know to be virtually useless. For students the pay-off is the qualification; for faculty a controllable and unchallenged encounter.

Although it seems plausible that some degree of cynicism of this sort can be found in management education, I doubt that it would survive and, indeed, grow if it were really so pointless. I think there *is* a point: the capacity of management education to socialize those subjected to it. The point is less the skills and knowledge it imparts and more its capacity to develop a certain kind of 'person', deemed to be suitable for managerial work and encultured into some version of managerial values. Indeed, it might be that the very willingness to undertake management education stands as a proxy (to employers) for a certain sort of orientation toward the world and commitment to its reproduction: a demonstration of being 'the right kind of person'. In this sense, management education may be taken as a symbolic indicator of possession of particular sorts of values, rather than possession of knowledge or skills. An interesting analogy is that of the accounting profession. Here, it is commonplace for firms to recruit accountancy graduates even though there are well-established data suggesting that such graduates perform, on average, less well in subsequent professional examinations than non-accountancy graduates. An empirical study of accounting firm recruitment showed that this was because hirers thought that accountancy graduates had shown an early commitment to the 'idea' of an accounting career and shown themselves to be the 'right kind of person', an attribute of considerable importance for fitting into, and advancing within, the profession.

My reasoning here is very much in line with what I said about the production of self-management in Chapter 3. Through socialization processes, which of course do not begin and end with management education, individuals acquire a view of what is normal and natural in the world – specifically, in this case, in relation to the world of organizations, and they position themselves and their behaviour accordingly. On this account, management education does have a functionality beyond the contract of cynicism, albeit one which is quite different to the conventional understanding of that functionality. In the latter, management education bestows skill as a bundle of techniques acquired by students for future deployment. In the former, management education develops the 'skill' of appropriate selfhood – a technique of self-construction and identity and value formation.

Such an understanding of management education is one which has considerable support from quite a variety of standpoints. Thus a leading US business school Dean likened (approvingly) the socialization processes of management education in the US to a 'bootcamp' and argues for the need to direct and enhance this socialization in evermore controlled ways (Leavitt, 1991). With considerably less approval, feminist scholarship has indicated the ways in which a masculinist set of values is built into management programmes and reproduced there (Sinclair, 1995). On this account, based on an empirical study in Australia, not only does management education validate values of control and domination, but it also uses case studies of predominantly male leaders and, in the classroom, routinely silences or discounts the contributions of female students.

Moving to a more general level, Whitley et al. (1981) analyse management education in terms of its relationship to wider structures of social inequality and elite reproduction. They found that MBAs (in particular) were increasingly forming an elite (and, of course, we would expect that process to have developed much further in the two decades since this study), which necessarily implies the formation of some shared set of values or understandings, since this is definitional to identifiable elites. All this does of course beg the question of whether management education – or even just the MBA – in general constitutes a common experience. After all, it might be that different programmes inculcate very different kinds of values and that we cannot speak of management education in the way that I have done. My sense is that there is less diversity than one might think – or hope – and that there are significant pressures against diversity. These come, in particular, from the growing importance of accreditation schemes and rankings or league tables (Wedlin, 2006). Such developments offer apparent guarantees of quality and transparent information, yet by definition they entail conformity to particular measures and, for that reason, homogenization. In any case, a key aspect of elite formation lies in one of the other relatively hidden aspects of management education: the way that it gives access to an alumni network of contacts. This aspect actually relies on a degree of heterogeneity, such that graduation from school X provides, uniquely, membership of school X's network.

Actually, it would be surprising if what I have said was wrong, because it is well known both that socialization is a facet of educational processes generally (Bowles and Gintis, 1976) and that high-level education is linked to the formation of social elites. In the UK, for example, it is possible to see a broad shift in the education of elites, from the study of classics as a prelude to colonial administration, to the study of social sciences as a prelude to entry into the bureaucracy of the welfare state, to the study of management as a prelude to entry into global corporations and consultancies. Clearly each of these represents a different mode of cultural reproduction and, hence, of socialization into different sets of behaviours, norms and values. This is indexed by the fact that one thing that management students often agree about is the way that their courses bestow a greatly enhanced sense of self-confidence upon those who take them. In terms of educational theory, management education offers individuals an entrée into a managerial 'habitus', or way of life, entailed within which is the possession of certain sorts of 'cultural capital' (Bourdieu, 1986) or social 'know-how'. This consists most clearly of habituation into the particular – and, for an outsider, peculiar – language of contemporary management practice. The capacity to talk and understand this language is a major accomplishment of management education. For business schools are one of the producers of managerial language, as well as being perhaps its most important distributor.

management education and legitimation

Habituation into managerial language is experienced as confidence enhancing for students, for obvious reasons. Anyone who has been abroad knows how confidence sapping it is to be unable to communicate. Management education offers entry into the language code of business, whether it be in terms of the latest jargon and buzz-words or the arcana of computing, accounting and finance. But there is more going on here than the development of individual confidence. Particularly within the context of global organization, a shared managerial language, as well as the values with which that language is associated, offers a basis for communication and trust even when conditions of work are fragmented spatially and temporally as in the 'post-bureaucracy' (Grey and Garsten, 2001). This kind of 'scripting' goes beyond language to the extent that it offers roles, orientations and a nascent sense of community. Moreover, because of the historically amassed status of universities, business schools are able to legitimate this language (etc.) by bestowing the hallmark of intel-lectualism, perhaps even science, as I suggested earlier.

It should, however, be recognized that not just *any* language will do. Indeed, more important than terminology are the ideological messages expressed through language and which remain relatively constant as business language changes. In general terms, management education acts to endorse both market relations and managerial dominance as normal, natural and inevitable features of social orga-nization and, more particularly, nowadays to promote the kind of fast capitalist story I discussed in Chapter 5 as normal, natural and inevitable (not least through the intense pressure on MBA programmes to be constantly busy). Management is often depicted as ideology-free technique; this is one of the legacies of understanding organizations simply in terms of formal rationality, as discussed in Chapter 1. I am a very long way from being the first person to question such a view, yet it continues to be standard in management programmes. Yet this very 'neutrality' is in fact political, for it is a way of concealing the inevitably value-laden terrain of organizations.

That this is so becomes obvious if we consider the way that the rise of management education in the UK was very closely related to the development of a politics which saw management and markets as preferable to unions and public provision. At the same time, education was seen more and more in vocational terms by politicians and, ulti-mately, by universities and students. The issues here go very deep, and are central to understanding the way management education works. Thomas Frank's excellent polemic, *One Market Under God* (2001) – from which I drew the opening quotation of this chapter – suggests that recent years have seen the advance of an ideology of 'market populism' in the US, UK and elsewhere. By this he intends not only the simple assertion of market primacy but also the linkage between markets and democracy. Under this ideology, markets represent the expression of popular will via the economic actions of individuals, and opposition to the market is therefore cast as anti-democratic and elitist, whether it is expressed by governments, intellectuals or professional groups. This is important because it advances a political and moral, as well as an economic, rationale for the market. Within this rationale, management thought occupies a very important place, Frank argues, for it legitimates corporate power. In particular, he singles out the breathless formulations of a new economy where organizations have souls and management is about informal partnership rather than domination.

Business schools, of course, have long been an important source, through research, of this kind of managerial thinking and, through management education, are certainly one of its key conduits. They are able to perform a sort of double movement. On the one hand, they bear the imprint of an engineering ideology that represents management as no more than morally neutral technique, as discussed in Chapters 1 and 2. On the other hand, they stand ready with an overtly moralistic stance in which the values of market populism and humanistic management are endorsed. And this should come as no surprise since the same duality has characterized much of the history of management thought, as I argued in Chapter 2. So – *and this is the key point* – in both versions, 'neutral' and 'humanist', stories such as that of the injection of amphetamines to prolong shifts are 'written out'. Neither the picture of the morally neutral technician nor of the morally inspired humanist could be sustained when confronted with this. And so management education either holds at a distance the real effects of, for example, neutral-sounding 'outsourcing' or condemns them as the reverse of good management practice – as anomalous events which can be easily dealt with by enlightened 'best practice'.

Business schools are therefore able to play a pivotal role in the ideological projects (note the pluralization) of globalized capitalism in promoting and, especially, socializing students into a sanitized representation of corporate management. That this should have occurred must be regarded as being at least in part serendipitous: it was not a part of a scheme or conspiracy. It *is* certainly true that there was a deliberate plan from the inception of business schools that they should raise the social status of business managers relative to established professional groups. Engwall (1997: 90) noted that for the many philanthropists who funded early business schools 'their intention was primarily to raise the status of business men' rather than having any particular concern with what was taught in the new institutions. For example, writing of Gustav Mevissen, creator of the business school at Cologne at the turn of the century, Robert Locke concluded that 'concerned to raise the low status of businessmen, he thought … to raise the businessman's social status by conferring college degrees on members of the business estate' (cited in Engwall, 1997: 91). This, of course, is a very different explanation of why management education emerged than that which sees it as to do with the functional need for better managers, and it is consistent with the arguments I made in Chapter 2 about the aspirations of management as an occupational group.

In this context the wider possibility of management education acting not just to boost the status of managers, but as a proselytizer and training ground for 'market populism' and for management as an 'idea', has emerged piecemeal. It may in part be due to the well-intentioned predisposition of academics in liberal cultures to articulate humane versions of what the organization is or should be. Yet these intentions cannot explain why, throughout the world, corporations and governments provide substantial financial support for business schools. Such support stems in part from the perceived need for the greater deployment of generic managerial skills in, especially, the public sector and management consultancies. This might initially be apprehended in terms of attempts to spread market discipline and 'business values', and this was probably true in the early periods of the New Right 'project'. However, it has subsequently taken on a distinct quality. As a term, 'generic management skills' itself implies the idea of management technique as a neutral artefact, ready to be put to use in pursuit of 'values' of all kinds, whether charity, health, banking or industry. But at the same time, in terms of 'market populism', it represents an incursion against supposedly entrenched privilege. Management is the way in which 'arrogant doctors' and public sector 'elites' may be made accountable. Yet there is an irony in this for, in the process, what is created is a new category of expert – the manager or the consultant – who, whilst not professionalized in the classical sense of the term, is possessed of techniques, language and values denied to others. In this sense it is right to cast management as a form of elitism even though part of its claim to value is anti-elitism.

I should reiterate that none of this is to posit a conspiracy or a simple alignment between management education and any particular set of interests. Debates in social theory have long emphasized the polymorphous nature of power and the fragmented character of interests (see Clegg, 1989). As with other institutions and social practices, management education operates within a complex terrain, and one growing more complex by virtue of the 'end of management' thesis I discussed in Chapter 5. This has lead to business schools increasingly positioning themselves as developing 'entrepreneurs', 'leaders' or, perhaps, 'change agents'. Nevertheless, their core operation remains the production of suitable personnel for, depending on their particular market, consultancies, investment banks, the public sector or industry. So, as a matter of expediency and not grand conspiracy, they must embody ideological positions which, at best, do not threaten the actual or perceived requirements of such employers who are often also involved in business school funding. However, the requirements of employers are themselves quite variegated: therefore it will not serve to see management education as the mouthpiece for a coherent, univocal set of interests. Indeed, aside from the issue of fragmentation of interests, business schools are themselves active players and as such cannot be understood simply as 'mouthpieces'.

Management education has had the good fortune to be carried by a tide of time and circumstance which have favoured it, rather than other forms of education or entitlement, to prosper. As the idea of management as a cultural good has been in the ascendant, so too has the demand for management education. As the hegemony of the market has been in the ascendant, so too has the demand for management education. Management education does not offer a useful 'technical' training, and nor could it. But, in purporting to do so, it does offer status and credentials to individuals and pre-selects and socializes those individuals for certain kinds of organizational employment. Through its socialization processes it contributes to the provision of shared languages and understandings amongst managers. It is therefore dependent upon wider cultural and political trends and can only be understood in the light of these. Moreover it offers some legitimation of those trends. It might, however, also be said that management education is as a result highly vulnerable to shifts in the ideological terrain or, perhaps more likely, in the value put upon general and generic management, especially by consultants and the public sector – hence, again, the increasing accent upon a different set of descriptors for what business schools offer.

Understood in this light, it is easy to understand why something like the 'Honduran story' – and more routine sweatshop practices – are so resolutely written out of management education. If management education is about status and legitimation, it must perforce be distanced from the more ethically dubious practices found in at least some real workplaces. Neither the status of managers nor the image of management as an idea are readily compatible with some of these practices, even though their existence suggests that they have an economic rationale. By the same token, the predominantly liberal-minded (in relative terms) faculty of business schools and, more certainly, the cultural capital of universities as sites of civilized values mitigate against overt endorsement of the increasing excesses of labour discipline in fast capitalism.

The analysis I am offering here differs more or less sharply from that provided by the more conventional critics of business schools (of whom there are many). Such criticism is now routine from within the heartlands of the business school mainstream as commentators such as Starkey and Tiratsoo (2007: 5) note. Of course the fact that the problematic nature of the business schools only receives much attention when it is articulated by the mainstream is another part of the problem, partly because it reflects a subservience to received wisdom. More importantly, it means that the critiques never radically reconsider the nature of business schools, so that they rather romantically imagine that the solution lies in making the business school more 'socially responsive'. A similar weakness can be found in the admittedly more intellectually sophisticated work of Rakesh Khurana (2007), which calls for more ethically-engaged and professionally-orientated (rather than simply market-focused) business schools. Whilst I have some sympathy for such analyses they are inevitably limited by an unwillingness to recognize the fundamental limitations of instrumental control and the nature of ideological co-option. Indeed, in terms of the latter, the call for a more ethical and socially responsive business school is simply to call for a re-enforcement of the role of business schools in ideological legitimation through an updated version of the humanistic part of that legitimation.

conclusion

The study of organizations nowadays takes place largely within the context of particular institutions, namely business and management schools. These schools have an interest in configuring organization theory in a particular way – as if it yields managerial control. That is, it says that studying organizations will make better, more professional managers. I have argued that this is a myth and that the real purpose of business schools is quite different, that it is about legitimation and status. For mainstream organization theory that doesn't make much difference, perhaps. It points to a body of work that emphasizes both the need to master it (status) and, over much of that work, the case for 'humanistic' management of the workforce (legitimation). Mastery of mainstream organization theory supports managers by suggesting that they both know more and are more humanely attuned than those who have not achieved such mastery. In this respect, modern business schools do no more than contribute to the ideological projects of managerial elitism referred to in the first two chapters of this book: the technical and ideological case for management.

However, using organization theory in this way can only work if an extremely partial and highly suspect approach is adopted. This approach stresses human behaviour as a variable that can be influenced by certain manipulations. This is evident in every mainstream discussion of organizations. Create motivational structure A and you will produce motivation level B. Use leadership approach A and you will produce organizational performance B. Create knowledge sharing system A and you will produce learning organization B. Such a view is commonly expressed by both instructors and students on management degrees as the provision of a 'toolkit' for managers; the very metaphor which betrays a mechanistic world view.

How inadequate this all is. I want to stress the inadequacy because the issue is not that this approach is heartless – but it works. The issue is that it doesn't work and cannot work. The entire notion of a toolkit requires that the objects to which the tools are applied are just that: objects. But they are not, they are people. So whilst this means that they should not be treated as objects, it also means that to do so will yield unsatisfactory results from a managerial perspective. For the agency of others means that the mastery of the manager will always and necessarily remain elusive. Concede this very basic insight, which appears to me unarguable, and the vast edifice of conventional organization theory is revealed as simple nonsense. All the regression analyses and hypothesis testing amount to no more than an elaborate game, requiring intelligence to play – and some of it is highly intelligent – but having no more meaning than a crossword puzzle. The only value it has is to contribute to the bigger project of the technical and ideological justification of management.

But if most studies of organization have this character, at once pointless and yet contributing to managerial ideology, why have I spent so much time urging the study of organizations? The answer is that although the mainstream has little value beyond 'the faking of intellectual authority', there is a considerable amount of organization theory that is of real value. It can tell us about the lived experience of organizations, and in this way illuminate our own and others' worlds. Which means that it can also be of value to professional managers not, as conventional wisdom would have it, by offering tools to control those around us, but by offering insights into why this controlling mentality is doomed to failure.

The way that the study of organizations is organized mitigates against that insight. For business schools purport to teach organization theory as a means of securing control. Rid ourselves of that presumption and we approach organization theory in a way which is more honest, more realistic and far more interesting. This observation brings me back to the issues with which I began the Introduction to this book. My concern there was that almost everything written about organization theory was terminally dull. I was puzzled by that, because I claimed that life in organizations was incredibly interesting. If you have followed me to this point then perhaps we have an explanation for my puzzlement. The way that the study of organizations has been subsumed into the narrow calculus of business school education explains why it has been denuded of everything that makes it interesting. If it is a tool of status and legitimation for managers, is it surprising that it speaks inadequately to our experience of going into work tomorrow?

So the professional managers produced by business schools are professional only in a very narrow – though not altogether insignificant – sense. They are not better or more effective managers or, if they are, only coincidentally. They may gain access to a network of alumni contacts but, if so, no more than they would had they spent the time studying something else. They may very well be more versed in the superficialities of managerial language, which may boost their self-confidence and, in some cases, their career prospects. But they will have learned something which fits them well for the corporate labour market over and above a language. They will have learned an orientation, and their study of organizations will have contributed to this. This orientation is, above and beyond everything else, an enrolment into or, perhaps especially for MBAs, a confirmation of a world view. That world view will typically encompass everything that this book has argued against. A view of organizations as a separate domain from that of philosophy, politics and culture. A view of organizations as amenable to engineering-like control. A view of people as a target for manipulation, and values as an organizational resource. A view of change as that which cannot be questioned, and must be enforced. A view that there is no alternative to fast capitalism.

So perhaps all this may be taken to mean that I am unsympathetic to business and management schools and their products. Well, yes, of course that is true. But unlike some advocates of 'critical management studies' (CMS) I heed the warning that:

> When the B-schools become empty, when the corridors contain dead leaves and the roofs leak, then they will be converted to sociology departments or housing for the elderly and CMS will have done its job [but] if the limit of your ambition is to put yourself out of a job, the prospects … do not seem to be bright. (Parker, 2002: 132)

That is not my ambition – either for myself or for business schools. Organizations are, and will likely remain, central to social and economic well-being in some form or other. But what form? I have taught many students over many years and my concern is that they are shortchanged. Many of them are talented, intelligent, ethical and likeable people who are fed a form of education that does little justice to these attributes. More fundamentally, I am convinced that organizations, and only organizations, can give us the many things that constitute the 'good life' in the way discussed at the end of Chapter 5. Business schools are a place where administration, politics, philosophy, ethics, psychology and much else of interest and importance can meet to contribute to the good life. My complaint is that by promoting a truncated version of organizational possibilities, these schools as currently constituted not only fail to contribute to the good life, but actively impede it.

Conclusion: Why Should Studying Organizations Matter to You?

*Necessity is the plea for every infringement of human freedom.
It is the argument of tyrants and the creed of slaves.*
William Pitt

Organizations matter because just about everything that we do occurs within an organization. The hospital where most of us are born, our playgroup, the doctor's surgery where we have our jabs, the infant, junior and secondary schools we attend, our university, our workplace, the government agencies which replace our hips and pay our pensions, the supermarkets where we shop, the banks and insurance companies we deal with, the travel agents and hotels which arrange our holidays, the media companies who provide our entertainment, the factories which make our cars and the garages which service them and provide their fuel, the coaches, trains and planes we use, the police and the army, the priest who buries us and the undertaker who digs our grave and provides the coffin: these are all organizational issues. How could organizations possibly not matter? We can all agree on that.

But this book has been concerned with a slightly different issue. Not organizations, as such, but *studying* organizations. This opens up the question of how we are to make sense of organizations. What concepts, ideas, theories, models and values are to be used not just to explain them but, often, to justify them or recommend their reform? This is the domain of organization theory. Now, for some, there may seem little difference between 'organizations' and 'studying organizations'. In the Introduction, I opened up the distinction between positivist and interpretivist or constructionist approaches to organization theory. For the positivists the relationship between organizations and studying organizations is, in principle, easy. All we need to do is to discover the facts of organizational life, no more and no less. In which case, why make life difficult for ourselves?

The problem, though, is that in organizations (and elsewhere in life) the facts do not speak for themselves. They are always interpreted and when the interpretations 'stick' and get believed by all or most people they become constructions. This issue can be seen even at the most basic level of defining what an organization is, as I discussed in Chapter 2 and again, in a different way, in Chapter 4.

Drawing the boundary is just that – drawing. We could include, say, pollution produced by a factory – or not; and this is not about facts but about interpretations. Does the factory end where its physical plant ends? Or does it end where the last molecule of its waste product is dispersed? Does it end when its workers sign off from their shift? Or does it end when the pissed-off worker finishes punching his wife's face? To those who confidently believe that the dividing line is self-evident I say: you mean that the interpretation of the dividing line is now so widely accepted as to be a construction.

If that argument is accepted then it follows that the construction (whatever it may be) is not *necessary*, in the sense of having to be that way, but contingent. It could be different. And for it to be different it must be reinterpreted. This is what gives the study of organization its importance, for it is crucially concerned with a contestation about what features of organizations will be noticed or ignored, emphasized or discounted, seen as important or dismissed as irrelevant. And to go back to my remarks in the Introduction about theory and practice, these interpretations are not just words or some separate domain from reality but are what determine what actually happens to people in the organizations which, we have agreed as common ground, are vitally important to everyone's lives.

For the bulk of mainstream organization theory the interpretation and construction of organizations is almost always refracted through the lens of efficiency. This feeds through into a whole host of other constructions with which this book has been concerned, but it is the stress on efficiency which is central. In this respect, organization theory owes much to economics but, again as I said in the Introduction, what I want to urge is a political rather than an economic understanding of organizations. For the focus on efficiency creates some insuperable problems. One, important, way of thinking about this goes right back to Max Weber's work with which I began Chapter 1. Weber's analysis of instrumental and substantive rationality marked a fault line in organization theory as well as being the originator of it as a 'subject'. The mainstream took instrumental rationality (or, for present purposes, efficiency) as being all that mattered; more critical approaches, such as mine, suggest that a focus on substantive rationality (for present purposes, politics, values and ethics) is the important issue.

From this perspective, the key question becomes: efficiency for whom? Traditional studies of organization only consider efficiency from the partial viewpoint of those who have an interest in a particular kind of efficiency. Normally this means the powerful – the people who own and run businesses being the obvious example. As soon as we shift position, efficiency can look quite different. Think of the now common way that all kinds of organizations use automated telephone systems, which I discussed in Chapter 4 in relation to customer focus. When we phone up, we are told to press different keys for different options and eventually, probably after waiting in a queue, we are connected to a call centre. Now this is efficient for the organization as it is a low-cost way of managing enquiries, partly because some of the work formerly done by an employee is now done, for nothing, by the caller. Sometimes, as with computer support lines, for example, the caller actually pays whilst they do this unpaid work for the organization. So from the caller's point of view it is not efficient because it involves a waste of time, sometimes a cost and, often, frustration. It also usually leads to a less personalized service (compare, for example, the traditional contact between a customer and a bank manager with that offered by national call centres).

I suggest that mainstream approaches to studying organizations have embodied a one-sided answer to questions of efficiency which is predominantly concerned with management.[1] That is, the managerial interpretation of organizations has become constructed as if it were an objective reality, so that we typically forget its constructed nature. It is a necessity – the way things have to be – rather than a contingency. This entire book has been concerned to offer an interpretation of organization theory which tries to unravel the partiality and assumptions of the orthodox approach.

As soon as we start to question what seem like self-evident ideas about organizations, then a much more complex picture emerges. This picture just won't allow us to talk in vague terms about efficiency and getting the job done as if these terms absolve us from ethical and political choices. By 'ethical' I don't mean anything very philosophical, just judgments about what is right and wrong. By 'political' I don't mean

---

1   To be sure, organization theory is only one aspect of this construction which fits into wider political and ideological constructs and contexts.

the politics of politicians and governments, or at least not exclusively so. I mean a wider sense of politics including the many ways that power is distributed and exercised, and the perpetual debates about, at the most general level, what to do and how to do it. My experience of management students, the most likely readers of this book, is that they often (but by no means always) hate this kind of talk. They don't want to think that managing organizations is about ethics and politics but would prefer to see it as about techniques, maybe even science, and regard any departure from this as an irrelevant waste of time. Well, sorry, but if you think this then you are wrong. What we do organizationally, including studying them, is always about ethics and politics. And, in a way, this is precisely because of the point with which I began this chapter. If so much of human life is organized, how could it be anything other than ethically and politically important? How could organizations inhabit some 'other world', separate from everything else? And isn't it ironic that those who adhere to such a view say that it describes the 'real world'?

I had a discussion with a student once and we were talking about scientific management. I was trying to say that efficiency might mean different things to different people. He agreed but then told me that this was 'just semantics' since what was *really* meant by efficiency was making the company more money. I asked him whether (in the context of Taylorism) it would seem to be 'just semantics' to be made to work harder or longer. My student didn't have an answer to that, but I could tell that he didn't really understand what I was asking. For him, it was obvious that making 'the company' more 'efficient' was plain reality and everything else was 'just semantics' (I guess he would have expressed it less politely behind my back).

One way of understanding conventional organization theory is that it proposes a particular set of answers to ethical and political dilemmas so that, for my student, these dilemmas just don't exist. For a focus on efficiency from the point of view of the powerful (I will discuss in detail later what I mean by this word), and on organization and management as technique, *is* such an answer. In its extreme form, it is an answer which says that the interests of the powerful are paramount, and that anything that they want to do, and can do, is fair enough (ethically, that would be to say something like 'might is right'). I disagree fundamentally with this, or more mild versions of the same argument (for example, to take a common variant, that the powerful can do whatever they like so long as it is legal). I am certainly not alone in that disagreement, but, it might be fairly said, so what? I'm free to disagree, so why go on about it?

I think there are good reasons why these arguments need to be made. One is a matter of general social responsibility. As I discussed in Chapter 1, extreme versions of this one-sided rationality of organizations lead to truly horrific consequences, with the Nazi Holocaust standing as the most awful example. Even if such situations don't currently seem to threaten, it is important always to remember that they can come into existence if we are not vigilant. Of course there were many reasons for Nazism and the Holocaust, most of which have little to do with organization theory. But the techniques of organization and in particular the blind pursuit of efficiency without regard to ethics were certainly two of the things which enabled the Holocaust and, more diffusely, the totalitarian management of the population at large. If we subscribe to the precepts of technique and efficiency and nothing else, then at the very least we have no defence against such events. I know that people sometimes think that invocations of Nazism and the Holocaust are overdone or inappropriate, and to some extent I agree, but it is important to recognize how these and other horrors define the ultimate limit of what is at stake when we discuss politics and ethics, and it would be more crass to ignore them than to address them.

Moreover, even though we may not currently seem to be in danger of totalitarian politics and genocide, that does not mean that organizations are not implicated within the production of same fairly major forms of suffering. As I suggested in the Chapter 6, the neutral sounding language of outsourcing and human resource management conceals some often appalling sweatshop labour practices. The fact that these may happen a long way from the countries where most of the corporate headquarters and business schools are located doesn't undermine the complicity of those institutions in the suffering which they create and support. And it is no good saying that these examples – of corporal punishment, bullying, illness and death – belong somehow to an outdated world of early industrialism. They do not. They belong to the present day and are geographically remote only because of the globalization that is blithely mentioned as part of the 'context' of modern management.

Often closer to home, as shown in Chapters 3 and 4, there are techniques of organizational control in the form of culture management and its derivatives which exert an insidious influence on people in organizations, attempting to manipulate their very sense of self. Perhaps these are not so alarming as the sweatshops; perhaps they are more so. It really depends on whether you would prefer to be coerced into doing something knowing it is coercion, or manipulated into something not realizing that it is manipulation. I'm not sure what the answer to this is, but neither seems particularly appealing. Then again, in Chapter 5 I tried to depict the world which, through organizations and management, we are in the process of creating: a world of time pressures, anxieties, indebtedness, declining social bonds and corporations which are animated more by short-term financial engineering than the long-term process of meeting human needs. Of course some readers will disagree with the way that I described that world, and I can accept that. But what it not acceptable would be to say that consideration of the world which organizations create is irrelevant to the study of organizations: not only is it relevant but it is central to what the entire purpose of such a study should be.

Second, beyond our general social responsibilities, these issues are particularly important to raise in the context of organization theory and management. A moment ago I said that conventional treatments of this subject could be seen as offering one kind of answer to political and moral issues, albeit one with which I disagreed. But it provides this answer in a very particular, and in my view entirely inadequate, way. It does it by pretending that the question does not exist. In other words, the assumptions about power, its distribution and its uses are presented as self-evident so that management is simply about technique.

One of the central ideas that informs the kind of work I do goes by the weighty name of 'de-naturalization' (Fournier and Grey, 2000). It means the attempt to expose and explain how those things which are taken to be natural or necessary – as 'just the way things are' and the way they need to be – are actually far from natural and are neither self-evident nor immutable. And this means that they never even get mentioned because why would anyone mention the patently obvious? But I think that it is *precisely* these 'obvious' things which need to be thought about. It is striking that although we live, as discussed in Chapter 4, in an era when everything is seen as changeable and up for grabs that there are so many things which are just assumed without question as immutable truths. Much of this book has been concerned with reinterpreting such supposed truths – about efficiency, personhood, choice, change and so on – in an attempt to show that they are contingent rather than necessary. If we realize that then new possibilities not just for thought but for action open up – for example in the ways that, as indicated in Chapter 5, the imperatives of fast capitalism can be questioned on grounds of the damage it does to individuals and communities so as to open up the alternatives that might exist in the form of 'slow life', environmentalism and localism. Again, you may think that these alternatives are undesirable, but this does not mean that discussion of what are desirable ways to live can be avoided when studying organizations.

The assumptions about power that I have referred to are, precisely, assumptions, but they are embedded into organization theory and either not mentioned or mentioned only in a cursory way. One aspect of this is the way that organization theory is, or has become, so closely associated with management, so that, as I have been at pains to indicate in this book, to write about the one is almost to write about the other. The assumption here, which is absolutely an assumption about power, is that organization must mean hierarchy and a division of labour between 'managers' and others, whether they be called workers, professionals, employees, team members or even partners. So one, very specific, form of organizing becomes 'naturalized' as if it were synonymous with organization. Yet management is very far from being a natural or inevitable feature of organizations, either in general terms or in the specific forms it takes.

There are many other such assumptions built into conventional organization theory, revolving around all the issues of efficiency, rationality, power and so on which I have tried to problematize in this book. It is these that, taken together, constitute the ethical and political issues which I am saying should be central to studying organizations. And when I say central, this means that it is not enough to treat these, as often now happens on management courses (although even this is belated and often begrudged), as 'optional extras' along the lines of business ethics or corporate governance and social responsibility. For one thing, such 'optional courses' are usually unwilling to probe the very fundamental ethical and political issues which I have argued are important. But, perhaps more importantly, and certainly relatedly, they fail to see how these fundamental issues are woven into the very fabric of organization theory and management.

To take an example which may clarify what I'm trying to get at, consider the issue of gender. Like business ethics, this has come somewhat onto the mainstream agenda of organizations, management and management education in recent years. Yet, like the bolt on ethics courses, they typically take the form of 'women in management', and discussions of, for example, the 'glass ceilings' which act as obstacles to women gaining senior positions in organizations. Now this isn't entirely without merit, I would be the first to agree. But what it doesn't touch on is the fundamental issue that, as many feminist writers such as Kathy Ferguson (1984) have argued, organization and management (and the bodies of theory which relate to them) are inherently masculinist. That is, the preoccupation with order, control, instrumental rationality, hierarchy and domination are attributes of, if not men, then masculinist apprehensions of how to be in the world. I have put this in very general terms, for what I am getting at is that, on this view, gender issues cannot be treated as secondary or additional but are absolutely centrally implicated. This exemplifies the wider[2] points I have made about the need to place ethics and politics at the centre of the study of organizations.

So, beyond whatever general responsibility there is for anyone to be attentive to the political and ethical issues embedded in organization, there is a particularly pressing reason why organization theory, organization theorists and students of organization theory should be so.

why 'why?' matters more than 'how?'

In this book I have tried to argue that organization theory should be concerned with much more than efficiency in the narrow sense. But I have also advanced what is perhaps a more radical argument. It is that not only does the focus on the primacy of efficiency ignore things which are more important but that, even within its own terms, it fails.

If this is true – and in a moment I will try to explain again why I believe that it is – then it represents a pretty damning indictment. For it would mean not only that organization theory doesn't do what I have

---

2   Wider in the sense that I have tried to problematize organization theory on a number of grounds, not just those relating to gender. Nevertheless, my arguments are, I think, often consistent with, and certainly informed by, feminist analysis.

argued it should do, but also that it doesn't even do what *it* says it should do. And it would also provide an answer to someone who had followed my arguments so far about how mainstream organization theory gives one kind of response to ethical and political issues, but who also agreed with that response and so would be quite happy just to get on with the pursuit of instrumental rationality in the service of the powerful. For of course this hypothetical person would be assuming that, within its narrow parameters, organization theory 'works'.

Now I have contended that there are not, and there cannot be, reliable organizational techniques if by that we mean actions (by managers, or others) which, if performed, will lead to predictable utcomes and only to those outcomes. Maybe this seems like a high hurdle to set, but it is precisely that promised by standard organization theory. If techniques don't produce predictable effects, then what would be the point of having them, since there would be no reason to think that following them would do what was wanted? And it must be the case that, if predictable outcomes are required, then this can be met if *only* those outcomes are produced. Otherwise, even if we had a technique which had *some* predictable outcomes, there would be no way of knowing whether the unpredicted outcomes were more detrimental (just from the narrow standpoint of efficiency) than the benefits of the predicted outcomes. I appreciate that this is convoluted, but it is important to establish exactly what we are talking about.

I have already indicated, at several points in this book, why such techniques do not exist. The core theoretical issues are those I talked about in Chapter 1: unintended consequences, agency and the impact of these upon predictability. In the natural sciences, for some and maybe many practical purposes, predictability is possible because we can design out unintended consequences and we are dealing with objects which don't have agency. In social things, including obviously organizations, this is not true because people do have some degree of agency, the variables surrounding their behaviour are too many and varied to be designed out and so predictions will not be reliable. And, as again was mentioned in Chapter 1, a particular feature of this is that the very fact of making predictions will set up the possibility that people will act differently precisely because of the predictions that have been made about them.

And this is not just true of 'people management' (which as I hope I showed in Chapter 2 is integrally and irreducibly contained within all modern conceptions of management). Even if we look at the supposedly hard, scientific aspects of management we find that there is no very good science. Thus, despite literally billions of pounds and literally billions of hours spent by hugely intelligent people trying to devise systems to beat the average of stock market performance, there is no system which in the long run is superior to making investments based upon random purchases of holdings.[3]

It is worth reflecting on what this means. As I suggested in Chapter 2, the conceit of people management is to draw into the managerial arena every feature of social life, a conceit extended in contemporary management theory and change management to attempts to mould people into a managerially acceptable shape. This opened up the idea that both the formal and informal organization could be managed. Yet what does such an idea amount to? The answer is very curious. If the formal organization is the overt, public, managed parts and the informal is the covert and spontaneous parts, then what the broad extension of management means is that the informal organization is itself manageable – that is, that the 'newly discovered' informal organization is *actually* subsumable into the formal.

This simultaneous separation and re-incorporation of the informal into the manageable is central to the modernist project of control and its contemporary extensions. By naming and charting the informal domain, this project renders that domain manageable, and has to, for otherwise control is not achievable. My thesis is that the informal always runs away from attempts to enclose it, for that is what informal organization means. So for every attempt to corral the informal into a managerial ambit, some new possibility opens up. In this sense management is a perennially failing operation, for each new domain into which it insinuates itself creates a new border beyond which it does not have purchase.

Thus scientific management attempted to destroy informal relations but, when these proved recalcitrant, the human relations approach opened up a way to manage rather than to destroy informality. But

---

3   Let me reiterate that what underlies this is that so-called 'management science' is *always* a version of 'people management'. The market is not an abstract entity but consists of a great many people moved by individual emotion, shared assumptions, group dynamics and even hysteria. Supposedly scientific models of these markets fail, not because they fail to recognize that it is people who inhabit financial markets but because they fail to recognize that these people can never be 'modelled'. Hence financial analysts always have recourse to cod psychology, e.g. market 'confidence'.

that approach, depending as it did on configuring human beings as fixed entities to be motivated, accommodated and worked around itself informed more recent attempts to shape and mould humanity through organizational culture. And these created costly commitments to providing a stable world for the new humans (for example, jobs for life) and so post-bureaucracy and its permanent flux of change morphing into an economy of permanent restructuring tries for the benefits of shaping people without the costs of doing so organizationally. That story could be told in many ways, and it isn't by any means the simple progression that I have depicted here. But the point is just that any attempt to managerialize – to define, compute and control – creates at the very point of that attempt the conditions for its own failure, so that the task of management is never done, and never could be done.

One reading of what I have said is that human beings will always find a way of subverting, of being outside of, the hand of management. I am inclined to think that this is true but not perhaps quite in the way that might be assumed. For to make such an assumption is to posit humanity as something which is ultimately knowable – perhaps in terms of thinking that there is a human spirit that makes them always want to resist. But this is not quite my view. In this book I have argued that any attempt to pin down what it is to be human is a contingent construction. The same is true of invocations of the human spirit. The point is not that I, or anyone, can know something about the nature of humans that means they subvert being managed but that there is an ultimate 'unknowability' which perpetually limits management.

How abstract and pointless all this will seem to the more hardheaded readers of this book. They are wrong. For the assumptions of the hard-headed are just as abstract, but are rarely stated. And if stated and explored they would reveal why management, and the organization theory that supports it, are so problematic. For their flaws explain why management continues in a blind circle of solution to problem to solution to problem. And there is no point in saying that, in that case, the pragmatic manager will have nothing to do with organization theory. As I said in the Introduction, any kind of organizational practice, such as managing, presupposes an organization theory. Choosing to hold and act upon an unexamined theory will not prevent the problems identified within an examined theory, it will just make the perpetual failures of organization and management even more inexplicable.

Those who have read so far may believe they have spotted an obvious flaw in my argument. Their analysis might run thus. Grey, poor sap, is hopelessly confused. On the one hand, he says that ignoring values and ethics in favour of efficiency can lead to the nightmare of the administrative 'perfection' of the Holocaust. On the other hand, he says that administrative perfection is impossible because of unintended consequences, agency and the ultimate unknowability of human beings and the ultimate uncontrollability of the informal organization. Which is it?

My answer is that it is both. When I say that organizations will always defy management control, I do not mean that they will totally do so. The death camps restricted massively the space for informal organization, unintended consequences and human possibility. Yet even there, these things persisted. Read Primo Levi's (1979) account of the way that some prisoners 'made out' ways of surviving or, perhaps even more noteworthy from the perspective of this book, the description of the Danish organization theorist Gunnar Hjelholt of his time in a Nazi concentration camp (Madsen and Willert, 1996). Even horrific attempts at manageability fail, but they are horrific for all that. Everyday attempts fail even more. So what I am saying is that conventional organization theory with its emphasis on control and efficiency leads at one extreme to horror and at the other extreme to failure. And these extremes are not just a matter of chance, but grow ineluctably out of the way that we habitually think about organizations and their management.

Now let me imagine a different kind of objection. What about a hospital, trying to save lives through medical care. Shouldn't this be run as efficiently as possible since any wasted resources will mean that someone who otherwise could be treated will die or suffer? Well, I agree – how could I not? But in this kind of case the organization is, presumably, animated by a substantively rational purpose (saving lives) and considerations of efficiency are in support of this purpose. There is nothing wrong with efficiency as a means if the end itself is justifiable in some other way that we agree is good. Of course in many cases there may be a disagreement about whether the purpose is good. Fine, but let's talk about that rather than assuming that efficiency is good in itself.

In any case, even in the hospital example, the nature of the purpose does not in itself undercut the concerns I have raised about efficiency. Let me give two kinds of example. First, many recent reforms of the UK National Health Service have been concerned to improves efficiency.

One way that this has been done is to reduce spare capacity in the system. This in turn has the effect that unusual peaks in demand, such as a major incident or a flu epidemic, swamp the system. My imaginary objection carried the implication that I would be heartless to decry efficiency in health care, but I could just as easily say that it is heartless to cause people to suffer in the name of efficiency. For the question still remains: efficient for whom? Is spare capacity inefficient from the point of view of the patient caught up in a demand peak? My second example is a much more extreme variant of a similar point. In 2004 a nurse in the UK was successfully prosecuted because she had encouraged the deaths of near-death patients on her ward, apparently as a way of freeing beds for those who needed them. Efficiency is always a negotiated and contestable concept, which depends on value judgments (for example, what is the relative importance of patients with quite near or very nearly terminal conditions?).

My quarrel with organization theory in the mainstream incarnation that is largely taught in management and business schools (and practised by managers and consultants) is that it doesn't give anything like enough attention, not just to these difficult cases, but to the underlying issues that affect all organizations. It consistently puts the cart before the horse by emphasizing the 'how' of organizations rather than the 'why'. And this can't be remedied by doing a little bit of 'why' after the 'how', because the 'how' always contains assumptions about the 'why'. That is, what should be the core of organization theory? The reasons, purposes or substantive rationality of organizations are, at best, the periphery; whilst the periphery of organization theory, the way they achieve these purposes or instrumental rationality, is almost always the core.

Now that observation brings us to what has been one of the major themes of this book. For I have not just been concerned with the *content* of organization theory but also its *context*. This came to the fore in Chapter 6, where I talked about business schools. These are the places where I, and most current-day organizational theorists, work and where you, in all likelihood, study. It is really impossible to understand the nature – and in my view deficiencies – of much organization theory without considering this context.

I have argued that the apparent purpose of business schools, to make their students better managers, is flawed. There is no evidence that they do. But this is not because they are engaged in any deliberate dishonesty, it is because they are an institutional expression of the failure of mainstream organization theory. That is, they subscribe to the dream of control without giving attention to the limitations of control I have identified in this book. You may be tempted to argue that organization theory is but one of the subjects of a management degree. But all of them – marketing, strategy, operations management, accounting and so on – are in different ways concerned with representing and intervening in organizations. Since these organizations are inhabited by people it follows that all the management subjects entail some kind of organization theory even if it isn't mentioned. Indeed, the less it is mentioned the more indefensible it is likely to be.[4]

Yet, although management degrees manifestly and necessarily fail to do what they claim, they are very popular. Why? Because actually they are not about training students in skills but in training them in orientation. This was my main point in Chapter 6. Business schools are not, currently, separate from the organizational world in the way that, for example, a politics department is (somewhat) separate from the political realm or a criminology department from the underworld. They are part and parcel of it. Which means that writing a book about organization theory that questions the tenets of the *subject* must also question the *institutions* within which that subject is taught. Which is what I have tried to do.

Conventional organization theory is the organization theory of business schools. However, the less conventional approach to organization theory that I have gestured towards in this book tells us something different. It tells us about the complexity of organizations, a complexity that makes them infinitely interesting. That, remember, was one purpose of this book – to say something interesting. Maybe I haven't succeeded, but even so it doesn't undercut the fact that organizations are interesting. They are interesting because it is never possible to say the final word about them. Because as human collectivities they contain all that is and could be human. Because, by doing so, they always defy complete description and control (or, to return to Chapter 2, representation and intervention). And this, which makes them interesting, is precisely what must be ignored by conventional, managerial representations of organization. For those representations *require* that organizations be nothing other than describable and controllable. So they must perforce suppress all the complexities which they do, in fact, contain.

---

4   Thus most management subjects simply assume that organizations are composites of rational individuals.

Those readers, the majority, who are studying management will, I think, know or at least sense that the stuff they learn is all about avoiding this complexity. It tries to contain reality into flow-charts, matrixes, four-by-four tables and so on. But those same readers will surely also know that their own experience – just like that of all the people who inhabit organizations – cannot be encapsulated in such banalities. All that is interesting escapes these codifications. Most courses on organization try to suppress these complexities – that is why they are boring. Recognize the complexities and, suddenly, organization theory becomes really interesting.

So why do I work in a business school, if all these places do is peddle a perverted version of organization theory and organizational life? In my darker moments I do not have an answer to this question, but I suppose it is because of the possibility of making a difference. Business schools offer a particular, perhaps unique, place where intellectuals (and I suppose I have to consider myself one, of sorts) can interact with society. There is no *necessary* reason why they should not offer an alternative understanding of the organizational world, and I have argued many times that there is a case for them to do so (e.g. Grey, 2004). For me to withdraw from them would represent a reduction – very small, but not absolutely negligible – in the likelihood of this happening.

but still, why should i care?

I don't think that anyone who needs an answer to this question will have read this far, but it is possible that someone may skip to this final passage of the book to try to see whether it has anything for them. Well, the answer to that question is not really to do with this book but to do with you, the person reading it. Ultimately, the way you respond to studying organizations depends upon two interrelated factors: the personal (or psychological) and the political. I'll take the latter first.

At the political level the question is the extent to which you accept current arrangements or think that they should change. My argument, especially in Chapter 6, has been that management education is geared towards the production of conformity. The imperatives of efficiency, competition, market relations and so on lead to the conclusion that organizations have of necessity to be the way they are. I think that this view is deeply unsatisfactory, not just because it occludes key questions (such as efficiency for whom?) but because it makes the frankly absurd assumption that the way that organizations are organized is efficient for anyone except a tiny minority. It isn't that organization theory delivers some way of organizing which is morally 'bad' yet managerially 'good'. What I have argued is that organization theory *does* deliver legitimation or justification for managers but *doesn't* reliably deliver effectiveness.

If that is right then we have to ask, what value should be put upon managerial legitimation? If you are a manager of a corporation then of course the answer is: quite a bit, thank you. But is that good enough? John Rawls (1972) in his magisterial *A Theory of Justice* proposes a very elegant way of assessing social arrangements, of which organizations are a prime example. In brief, he asks what arrangements would be agreed to by people behind a 'veil of ignorance'. This means: what would people agree to if they did not know their gender, race, place in the hierarchy, bodily ability and so on? In the wider social sense Rawls argues that people would not agree to arrangements that substantially disadvantaged any one group, given that they did not know what group they would belong to.[5] In the organizational context it means that we might be unwilling to give pre-eminence to managerial interests given that we cannot know (from behind the veil of ignorance) whether these interests will be our own.

Rawlsian concepts of justice allow us to decouple organizational relations from interests. Given that most management students will be actual or aspirant managers, this is helpful in establishing an approach to organization theory which is detached from managerial interests. The entire tenor of managerialist thought is to propose that what is good for one is good for all. Why should such a constricted set of ideas about organizations be taken as organization theory? Only because the powerful have found it useful to them to do so. Ignore the interests of the powerful, as the Rawlsian veil of ignorance allows us to do, and things look very different. I would be surprised if anyone, not knowing whether they would be one of 'them' or not, would be happy to agree to an organizational world in which, to go back to a passage I quoted in Chapter 3, 'The idea is to educate people without them knowing it. Have the religion and not know how they got it' (Kunda, 1992: 5).

---

5 Astute readers will note that Rawls's theory of justice is in effect a restatement of the Kantian categorical imperative outlined in Chapter 1. However, the striking 'veil of ignorance' metaphor is a good way of operationalizing Kantian ethics.

However, Rawls's formulation, although helpful in thinking about interests, does not go far enough. Despite my talk here and elsewhere in this book about 'the powerful', power is far more complex than such talk would suggest. We cannot see the world in terms of oppressors and victims or managers and workers because each of these is both implicated in, and produced through, power relations. An example, mentioned in Chapter 3, is the way that ludicrously hardworking managers and professionals are themselves fostered by organizational regimes that promote a sense of self-managed responsibility.

In this sense, my analysis of organization theory is different to the traditional left-wing complaint about the oppression and exploitation of workers, such as has been associated with traditional critiques from, in particular, labour process analysis (Braverman, 1974). For my belief is that organization theory subjugates almost all of us and, indeed, that the relatively petty differences between 'workers' and 'managers' leads to the latter being terrified to question the established order for fear of losing their small advantages. Better to read the *Daily Mail* and bemoan the fecklessness of the unions.

I don't mean by this that I don't understand the difference in life experience between a sweatshop worker in a shoe factory in the Philippines working massive hours for a pittance, and a middle manager of a footwear conglomerate, living in a British commuter village, stressed out by the endless demands for cost savings and fearful of the next round of downsizing. In a real material sense, the former is much worse off than the latter. It's just that I see them as both locked within a common understanding of organizations, and locked within it whether they agitate for more from, or devise ways of giving less to, each other. Indeed, I think that only by recognizing their interdependence can any real progress be made. And that interdependence is masked by conventional organization theory because just as it makes the Philippino worker the object of the British manager's efficiency gain, it tries to make that manager the slave of the corporate imperatives of the organization that employs them both.

In Chapter 5 I tried to draw out the implications of all this by discussing the nature of contemporary society. This society is characterized by a 'fast capitalism' in which organizations are sites not primarily for delivering goods and services but for a financial engineering which demands endless restructuring and more and more intense work. The fundamental question we have to ask is: why? Who is this good for? It propels us into a world not just of ever-greater stress but also one which undermines social and communal bonds. It detaches organizations from places and people and in return delivers an economic growth which does not make people happy – and perhaps makes people less happy – even when it sometimes makes them richer, and which is deleterious to the environment as well as to social well-being. It places us on a lifelong and ever-faster spinning hamster wheel of work, debt and consumption.

Ultimately, then, we have to take a stance on the politics of all this. But our capacity to do so is also about our personal or psychological commitments. These are not separate things. Traditional socialist takes on these issues assumed that the issues were objective. The oppressed worker in the Philippines or anywhere else would have a natural interest in challenging the power of the multinational, just as the financier in London or anywhere else would have a natural interest in supporting that power. Nonsense. The worker might well be dreaming of and working towards the day when she or he had saved up enough money to set up their own business, or for their child to do so or, who knows, for their child to attend a business school! The financier might well dream of having the courage to depart the 'rat race' and raise chickens on an organic freeholding. Although their experiences, choices and material prosperity are very different, both of these hypothetical people are linked in a systemic way.

The word 'systemic' is important here, because it suggests that there is much more at stake here than the individual choices which people can (or cannot) make within the system in which they operate. And one part – minor for sure but not entirely insignificant – of that system is the institutions where organizations and management are studied. At the moment, I think that these institutions do a generally poor job of dealing with what is at stake in such study, but as with everything I have said in this book up to now, I do not think there is any necessity here. It seems to me perfectly possible that the manager or aspirant manager can take a non-managerialist view, and certainly that organizations can be about more than instrumental rationality. I would hardly have written this book if I did not believe this to be so. However, my experience is that far too many managers and management students (and, indeed, others) like the certainties of the conventional approach. Too many buy into macho management because more fundamentally they buy into the idea that caring about others is wimpy. Too many embrace selfishness because they have yet to experience profoundly, and ignore their daily experiences of, dependence on others. Too many embrace certainty because they are terrified by its alternative. Too many lack imagination, empathy and insight into others, so it is small wonder they embrace the truncated, stunted and callous version of organization theory against which I have been arguing. However, it is surely also the case that many managers, students and others do not lack imagination, empathy and insight, and for them the issue is rather that the way in which they are encouraged to study organizations gives little or no space for them to understand how it can be wider, richer and more engaged.

Studying organizations is inseparable from political choices. In mainstream approaches, these choices are largely ignored when it is assumed that organizations are, and should be no more than, sites of instrumentally rational control. What a deficient and damaging view of life that is – as damaging to those who hold it almost as much as it is to everyone else. But aside from the deficiencies are the absurdities. For even within that narrow view what is abundantly clear is that organizations cannot be controlled that way. And what is at stake when we study organizations is not words on a page, but the way in which these relate to and inform actions that impact upon the world in terms of the way people are treated at work, the way that we provide for ourselves and others, and the consequences of this for the environment and for social well-being.

So that, finally, is the issue. The stakes are very high. What kind of world do you want? It has to be an organizational world for, so far as I can see, there is no other on offer. The choice is both political and personal. Politically, the world offered by conventional organization theory is hideously distorted by managerialism in the sense that it treats managerial concerns and realities as being identical with what is true of organizations in general. It ignores all the consequences of organizations except for those that figure in a narrow calculus of a one-sided notion of efficiency. Personally, the world offered by conventional organization theory appeals only to those willing to distort themselves and others in line with stunted notions of people as controlled and controlling at the expense of the true range of their human potentials. Truth is always elusive, but the manifest distortions entailed by both of these positions make it self-evident to me that they cannot be true. The purpose of this short book has been to say some things about the study of organizations which seem to me to be true.

Recommended Reading

Eleven books I would recommend on the things discussed in this book:

Anthony, P. (1977) *The Ideology of Work*. London: Routledge.

Bauman, Z. (1989) *Modernity and the Holocaust*. Cambridge: Polity.

Burrell, G. (1997) *Pandemonium*. London: Sage.

du Gay, P. (2000) *In Praise of Bureaucracy*. London: Sage.

Jacques, R. (1996) *Manufacturing the Employee*. London: Sage.

Locke, R. (1996) *The Collapse of the American Management Mystique*. Oxford: Oxford University Press.

Parker, M. (2002) *Against Management*. Cambridge: Polity.

Rose, N. (1989) *Governing the Soul*. London: Routledge.

Sennett, R. (2006) *The Culture of the New Capitalism*. New Haven, CT: Yale University Press.

Shenhav, Y. (1999) *Manufacturing Rationality*. Oxford: Oxford University Press.

Weil, S. (1988) *Oppression and Liberty*. London: Ark. (*Oppression et Liberté*. Paris: Gallimard, 1955 [orig. 1933])

References

Aldrich, H. (1979) *Organizations and Environments*. Englewood Cliffs, NJ: Prentice-Hall.

Alvesson, M. and Willmott, H. (eds) (1992) *Critical Management Studies*. London: Sage.

Association of Business Schools (2008) *Pillars of the Economy*. Available at www.the-abs.org.uk/files//PILLARSandAR.pdf. Accessed 15 February 2008.

Augé, P. (1995) *Non-places: Introduction to an Anthropology of Supermodernity*. London: Verso.

Baritz, S. (1960) *Servants of Power*. Middletown: Wesleyan University Press.

Basso, P. (2003) *Modern Times, Ancient Hours: Working Lives in the 21st Century*. London: Verso.

Bauman, Z. (1989) *Modernity and the Holocaust*. Cambridge: Polity.

Bauman, Z. (2000) *Liquid Modernity*. Cambridge: Polity.

Berry, A., Capps, T., Cooper, D., Tinker, T. and Lowe, E. (1987) 'The ethics of research in a public enterprise', in F. Heller (ed.), *The Uses and Abuses of Social Science*. London: Sage. pp. 85–98.

Beynon, H. (1973) *Working for Ford*. London: Penguin.

Blau, P. (1955) *The Dynamics of Bureaucracy*. Chicago: Chicago University Press.

Boltanski, L. and Chiapello, E. (2007) *The New Spirit of Capitalism*. London: Verso.

Bourdieu, P. (1986) *Distinction. A Social Critique of the Judgement of Taste*. London: Routledge & Kegan Paul.

Bourdieu, P. (ed.) (1999) *The Weight of the World. Social Suffering in Contemporary Society*. Cambridge: Polity.

Bowles, S. and Gintis, H. (1976) *Schooling in Captalist America*. London: Routledge & Kegan Paul.

Braverman, H. (1974) *Labor and Monopoly Capital*. New York: Monthly Review Press.

Brocklehurst, M., Grey, C. and Sturdy, A. (2007) 'Management: The Work that Dares Not Speak its Name', Working Paper (Unpublished).

Burnham, J. (1945) *The Managerial Revolution*. London: Penguin.

Burrell, G. (1988) 'Modernism, postmodernism and organizational analysis: the contribution of Michel Foucault', *Organization Studies*, 9 (2): 221–35.

Carnall, C. (1995) *Managing Change in Organizations*. London: Prentice-Hall.

Casey, C. (2002) *Critical Analysis of Organizations*. London: Sage.

Caulkin, S. (2007) 'How ICI settled on the wording of its epitaph', *Observer*, 24 June. Available at http//observer.guardian.co.uk/business/story/0,,2109728,00.htm. Accessed 24 June 2007.

Chrisafis, A. (2003) 'Fiascos that haunt "can do" company' *Guardian*, 15 February.

Clegg, S. (1989) *Frameworks of Power*. London: Sage.

Crenson, M. (1971) *The Unpolitics of Air Pollution*. Baltimore: Johns Hopkins Press.

Crosby, P. (1979) *Quality is Free*. New York: McGraw-Hill.

Crozier, M. (1964) *The Bureaucratic Phenomenon*. Chicago: University of Chicago Press.

Daintith, J. (ed.) (2000) *Quotations for Speeches*. London: Bloomsbury.

Dalton, M. (1959) *Men who Manage*. New York: John Wiley & Sons.

Delbridge, R. (1998) *Life on the Line in Contemporary Manufacturing*. Oxford: Oxford University Press.

DiMaggio, P. and Powell, W. (1983) 'The iron cage revisited: institutional isomorphism and collective rationality in organizations', *American Sociological Review*, 48: 147–60.

Drucker, P. (1955) *The Practice of Management*. London: Heinemann.

du Gay, P. (2000) *In Praise of Bureaucracy: Weber, Organization and Ethics*. London: Sage.

du Gay, P. (2003) 'The tyranny of the epochal: change, epochalism and organizational reform', *Organization*, 10 (4): 663–84.

Edwards, R. (1979) *Contested Terrain: The Transformation of the Workplace in the Twentieth Century*. London: Heinemann.

Ehrenreich, B. (2006) *Bait and Switch: The Futile Pursuit of the Corporate Dream*. London: Granta.

Elliott, L. and Atkinson, D. (2007) *Fantasy Island*. London: Constable Robinson.

Engwall, L. (1997) 'Mercury and Minerva: a modern multinational academic business studies on a global scale', in J.L. Alvarez (ed.), *The Diffusion and Consumption of Business Knowledge*. London: Macmillan, pp. 81–109.

Engwall, L. and Zamagni, V. (eds) (1998) *Management Education in Historical Perspective*. Manchester: Manchester University Press.

Ferguson, K. (1984) *The Feminist Case against Bureaucracy*. Philadelphia, PA: Temple University Press.

Fineman, S. (1996) 'Emotion and organizing', in S. Clegg, C. Hardy and W. Nord (eds), *The Handbook of Organization Studies*. London: Sage, pp. 543–64.

Fletcher, C. (1973) 'The end of management', in J. Child (ed.), *Man and Organization*. London: Allen & Unwin. pp. 135–57.

Folkman, P., Froud, J., Johal, S. and Williams, K. (2006) 'Working for themselves? Capital market intermediaries and present day capitalism', *Centre for Research on Socio-Cultural Change Working Paper 25*. Milton Keynes: Open University.

Foucault, M. (1979) *Discipline and Punish*. London: Penguin.

Foucault, M. (1991) 'Governmentality', in G. Burchell, C. Gordon and P. Miller (eds), *The Foucault Effect. Studies in Governmentality*. London: Harvester Wheatsheaf, pp. 87–104.

Fournier, V. and Grey, C. (2000) 'At the critical moment: conditions and prospects for critical management studies', *Human Relations*, 53 (1): 7–32.

Frank, T. (2001) *One Market Under God*. London: Weidenfield & Nicolson.

Freedman, R. (ed.) (1962) *Marx on Economics*. London: Pelican.

Fromm, E. (1942) *Fear of Freedom*. London: Routledge & Kegan Paul.

Froud, J., Johal, S., Leaver, A. and Williams, K. (2006) *Financialization and Strategy: Narratives and Numbers*. London: Routledge.

Gee, J., Hull, C. and Lanshear, C. (1996) *The New Work Order: Behind the Language of the New Capitalism*. Sydney: Allen & Unwin.

Gewirtz, S. (2002) *The Managerial School*. London: Routledge.

Giddens, A. (1984) *The Constitution of Society*. Cambridge: Polity.

Gouldner, A. (1954) *Patterns of Industrial Bureaucracy*. New York: Free Press.

Grey, C. and Garsten, C. (2001) 'Trust, control and post-bureaucracy', *Organization Studies*, 22 (2): 229–50.

Grey, C. (1996) 'Towards a critique of managerialism: the contribution of Simone Weil', *Journal of Management Studies*, 33 (5): 591–611.

Grey, C. (1999) 'We are all managers now, we always were. On the development and demise of management', *Journal of Management Studies*, 36 (5): 561–86.

Grey, C. (2004) 'Reinventing business schools: the contribution of critical management education', *Academy of Management Learning and Education*, 3 (2): 178–86.

Grey, C. and Sinclair, A. (2006) 'Writing differently', *Organization*, 13 (3): 443–53.

Grey, C. and Willmott, H. (eds) (2005) *Critical Management Studies: A Reader*. Oxford: Oxford University Press.

Grint, K. (1997) *Fuzzy Management*. Oxford: Oxford University Press.

Hacking, I. (1983) *Representing and Intervening*. Cambridge: Cambridge University Press.

Hacking, I. (1991) 'How should we do the history of statistics?', in G. Burchell, C. Gordon and P. Miller (eds), *The Foucault Effect. Studies in Governmentality*. London: Harvester Wheatsheaf, pp. 181–96.

Hammer, M. and Champy, J. (1993) *Reengineering the Corporation: A Manifesto for Business Revolution*. London: Nicholas Brealey.

Hancock, P. (2006) 'The spatial and temporal mediation of social change', *Journal of Organizational Change Management*, 19 (5): 619–39.

Hancock, P. and Tyler, M. (eds) (2008) *The Management of Everyday Life*. Basingstoke: Palgrave.

Harding, N. (2003) *The Social Construction of Management*. London: Routledge.

Harvey, D. (1989) *The Condition of Postmodernity*. Oxford: Blackwell.

Heckscher, C. (1994) 'Defining the post-bureaucratic type', in C. Heckscher and A. Donnellon (eds), *The Post-bureaucratic Organization: New Perspectives on Organizational Change*. Thousand Oaks, CA: Sage, pp. 14–62.

Heckscher, C. (1995) *White Collar Blues*. New York: Basic Books.

Hirst, P. and Thompson, G. (1996) *Globalization in Question*. Cambridge: Polity.

Hochschild, A. (1997) *The Time Bind: When Work Becomes Home and Home Becomes Work*. New York: Metropolitan Books.

Honoré, C. (2004) *In Praise of Slow*. London: Orion.

Huxley, A. (2006/1932) *Brave New World*. New York: Harper Collins.

Jacques, R. (1996) *Manufacturing the Employee. Management Knowledge from the 19th to the 21st Centuries*. Thousand Oaks, CA: Sage.

James, O. (2007) *Affluenza*. London: Random House.

Kamata, S. (1982) *Japan in the Passing Lane: An Insider's Account of Life in a Japanese Auto Factory*. New York: Pantheon.

Kanter, R.M. (1977) *Men and Women of the Corporation*. New York: Basic Books.

Khurana, R. (2007) *From Higher Aims to Hired Hands: The Social Transformation of American Business Schools and the Unfulfilled Promises of Management as a Profession.* Princeton, NJ: Princeton University Press.

Klein, N. (2000) *No Logo.* London: Flamingo.

Knights, D. (1992) 'Changing spaces: the disruptive impact of a new epistemological location for the study of management', *Academy of Management Review*, 17: 514–36.

Koch, R. and Godden, I. (1996) *Managing without Management: A Post-management Manifesto for Business Simplicity.* London: Nicholas Brealey.

Kodz, J., Davis, S., Lain, D., Strebler, M. and Rick, J. (2003) *Working Long Hours: A Review of the Evidence.* DTI Employment Relations Research Series, ERRS16. London: HMSO.

Kummer, C. (2002) *The Pleasures of Slow Food: Celebrating Authentic Traditions, Flavors and Recipes.* San Francisco: Chronicle.

Kunda, G. (1992) *Engineering Culture.* Philadelphia, PA: Temple University Press.

Lash, S. and Urry, J. (1994) *Economies of Signs and Space.* London: Sage.

Layard, R. (2005) *Happiness: Lessons from a New Science.* London: Penguin.

Leadbetter, C. (1999) *Living on Thin Air.* London: Hodder & Stoughton.

Leavitt, H. (1991) 'Socializing our MBAs: total immersion? managed culture? brainwashing?', *California Management Review*, 33 (4): 127–43.

Levi, P. (1979) *If This is a Man/The Truce.* London: Penguin.

Lewin, C. (1951) *Field Theory in Social Science.* New York: Harper & Row.

Locke, R. (1996) *The Collapse of the American Management Mystique.* Oxford: Oxford University Press.

Lukes, S. (1974) *Power: A Radical View.* London: Macmillan.

Luttwak, E. (1999) *Turbocapitalism: Winners and Losers in the Global Economy.* New York: Harper Collins.

MacIntyre, A. (1981) *After Virtue.* London: Duckworth.

Madsen, B. and Willert, S. (1996) *Survival in the Organization. Gunnar Hjelholt Looks Back at the Concentration Camp from an Organizational Perspective.* Aarhus, Denmark: Aarhus University Press.

Mant, A. (1977) *The Rise and Fall of the British Manager.* London: Macmillan.

March, J. (2000) 'Plenary Address', 16th EGOS Colloquium, Helsinki, Finland, July 2–4.

Meek, V. (1988) 'Organizational culture: origins and weaknesses', *Organization Studies*, 9 (4): 453–73.

Merkle, J. (1980) *Management and Ideology*. Berkley, CA: University of California Press.

Merton, R. (1940) 'Bureaucratic structure and personality', *Social Forces*, May: 560–8.

Minns, R. (2001) *The Cold War in Welfare: Stock Markets versus Pensions*. London: Verso.

Mumford, L. (1967) *The Myth of the Machine, Volume 1: Technics and Human Development*. San Diego: Harcourt Brace Jovanovich.

Naish, J. (2008) *Enough: Breaking Free from the World of More*. London: Hodder & Stoughton.

National Audit Office (2002) 'Individual Learning Accounts' (Press Notice 60/02). Available at www.nac.org.uk/pn/ø1-ø2/ø1ø21235.ntm. Accessed 13 June 2008.

Ogbonna, E. and Wilkinson, B. (1988) 'Corporate strategy and corporate culture: the view from the checkout', *Personnel Review*, 19 (4): 9–15.

Orwell, G. (1946) 'James Burnham and the managerial revolution', *New English Weekly*, May. Available at www.k-1.com/Orwell/site/work/essays/burnham.html. Accessed 17 January 2008.

Orwell, G. (1949) *Nineteen Eighty-four*. London: Secker & Warburg.

Parker, M. (2002) *Against Management*. Cambridge: Polity.

Parker, S., Brown, R., Child, J. and Smith, M. (1977) *The Sociology of Industry*. London: Allen & Unwin.

Pascale, R. and Athos, A. (1982) *The Art of Japanese Management*. London: Penguin.

Perelman, M. (2005) *Manufacturing Discontent: The Trap of Individualism in Corporate Society*. London: Pluto.

Peters, T. and Waterman, R. (1982) *In Search of Excellence*. New York: Harper & Row.

Petrini, C. (2001) *Slow Food: Collected Thoughts on Taste, Tradition, and the Honest Pleasures of Food*. White River Junction, VT: Chelsea Green.

Pollard, S. (1965) *The Genesis of Modern Management*. London: Penguin.

Putnam, R. (2000) *Bowling Alone*. New York: Simon & Schuster.

Rawls, J. (1972) *A Theory of Justice*. Oxford: Oxford University Press.

Reiss, H. (ed.) (1991) *Kant. Political Writings*. Cambridge: Cambridge University Press.

Roberts, J. (1984) 'The moral character of management practice,' *Journal of Management Studies*, 21 (4): 287–302.

Roberts, J. and Armitage, J. (2006) 'From organiation to hypermodern organization: the accelerated appearance and disappearance of enron', *Journal of Organizational Change Management*, 19 (5): 558–77.

Rose, N. (1989) *Governing the Soul*. London: Routledge.

Rosen, M. (1988) 'You asked for it: Christmas at the bosses' expense', *Journal of Management Studies*, 25 (5): 463–80.

Russell, B. (1935/2001) *In Praise of Idleness*. London: Routledge.

Schwartz, B. (2004) *The Paradox of Choice: Why More is Less*. New York: Harper Perennial.

Schwartzman, B. (1993) *Ethnography in Organizations*. Qualitative Research Methods Series No. 27. Newbury Park, CA: Sage.

Semler, R. (1993) *Maverick*. London: Century.

Senge, P. (1993) *The Fifth Discipline*. London: Random House.

Sennett, R. (1998) *The Corrosion of Character: The Personal Consequences of Work in the New Capitalism*. New York: Norton.

Sennett, R. (2006) *The Culture of the New Capitalism*. New Haven, CT: Yale University Press.

Sewell, G. and Wilkinson, B. (1992) 'Someone to watch over me: surveillance, discipline and the just-in-time labour process', *Sociology*, 26 (2): 271–89.

Shenhav, Y. (1999) *Manufacturing Rationality*. Oxford: Oxford University Press.

Sinclair, A. (1995) 'Sex and the MBA', *Organization*, 2 (2): 295–317.

Smircich, L. (1983) 'Concepts of culture and organizational analysis', *Administrative Science Quarterly*, 28: 339–58.

Starkey, K. and Tiratsoo, N. (2007) *The Business School and the Bottom Line*. Cambridge: Cambridge University Press.

Stewart, T.A. (1993) 'Reengineering: the hot new managing tool', *Fortune*, 128 (4): 32–7.

Strange, S. (1986) *Casino Capitalism*. Oxford: Basil Blackwell.

Strathern, M. (ed.) (1992) *Audit Culture: Anthropological Studies in Accountability, Ethics and the Academy*. London: Routledge.

Thomas, R. and Dunkerley, D. (1999) 'Careering downwards? Middle management in the downsized organization', *British Journal of Management*, 10 (2): 157–69.

Thrift, N. (2005) *Knowing Capitalism*. London: Sage.

Tienari, J. (2006) 'Critical thinking, no fancy word play [Review of *a very short, fairly interesting and reasonably cheap book about studying organizations* by Chris Grey]', *Organization*, 13 (2): 302–3

Useem, M. (1984) *The Inner Circle: Large Corporations and the Rise of Business Political Activity in the US and UK*. Oxford: Oxford University Press.

Virilio, P. (1977) *Speed and Politics: An Essay on Dromology*. New York: Semiotext(e).

Voltaire, F. (2001/1759) *Candide*. London: Penguin.

Vroom, V. (1964) *Work and Motivation*. New York: John Wiley.

Warhurst, C. and Thompson, P. (1998) 'Hands, hearts and minds: changing work and workers at the end of the century', in P. Thompson and C. Warhurst (eds), *Workplaces of the Future*. Basingstoke: Macmillan, pp. 1–24.

Watson, T. (1996) 'Motivation: that's Maslow isn't it?', *Management Learning*, 27 (4): 447–64.

Wedlin, L. (2006) *Ranking Business Schools*. Chelterhem UK: Edward Elgar.

Weil, S. (1949) *L'Enracinement: Prélude á une déclaration des devoirs envers l'être humain*. Paris: Gallimard. [Translated as *The Need for Roots*. New York: Putnam, 1952].

Wheatley, M. (1992) *The Future of Management*. Corby: British Institute of Management.

Whitley, R., Thomas, A. and Marceau, J. (1981) *Masters of Business. The Making of a New Elite?* London: Tavistock.

Willmott, H. (1993) 'Strength is ignorance, slavery is freedom: managing culture in modern organizations', *Journal of Management Studies*, 30 (5): 515–52.

Index

Research Methods Books from SAGE

Basics of QUALITATIVE RESEARCH 3e

Juliet Corbin
Anselm Strauss

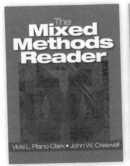

The Mixed Methods Reader

Vicki L. Plano Clark • John W. Creswell

DOING QUALITATIVE RESEARCH USING YOUR COMPUTER

A PRACTICAL GUIDE

CHRIS HAHN

SECOND EDITION
INTERVIEWS
Learning the Craft of Qualitative Research Interviewing

Steinar Kvale
Svend Brinkmann

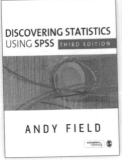

DISCOVERING STATISTICS USING SPSS THIRD EDITION

ANDY FIELD

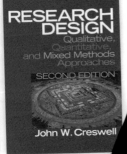

RESEARCH DESIGN
Qualitative, Quantitative, and Mixed Methods Approaches

SECOND EDITION

John W. Creswell

The Qualitative Research Kit

Edited by Uwe Flick

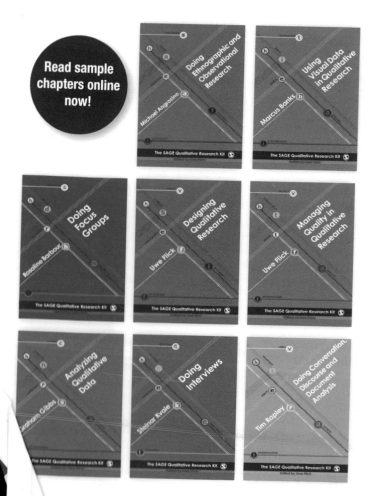

Read sample chapters online now!

Doing Ethnographic and Observational Research — Michael Angrosino

Using Visual Data in Qualitative Research — Marcus Banks

Doing Focus Groups — Rosaline Barbour

Designing Qualitative Research — Uwe Flick

Managing Quality in Qualitative Research — Uwe Flick

Analyzing Qualitative Data — Graham Gibbs

Doing Interviews — Steinar Kvale

Doing Conversation, Discourse and Document Analysis — Tim Rapley

The SAGE Qualitative Research Kit

gepub.co.uk